CHRIST THE WORD

BY

PAUL ELMER MORE

GREENWOOD PRESS, PUBLISHERS
NEW YORK

PREFACE

WITH this volume the historical study of the Greek Tradition is brought to a close, the long journey *per tot discrimina rerum,* from the death of Socrates to the Council of Chalcedon, just eight and a half centuries to the year, is ended.

I call the work historical, yet perhaps I should say again that it is so only in a liberal sense of the word. Particularly in the present case, though the treatment is chronological, there has been no attempt to give a full and connected account of the literature under consideration, but the material has been chosen and the discussion directed with a single thesis in view. The book is thus rather a monograph than a history. Such a method has seemed to me justifiable because the whole course of Greek theology itself, though it branched off into innumerable minor issues, was steadily centred upon the one question of the authenticity and meaning and consequences of the Incarnation.

In my insistence on the primacy of this thesis it may appear that I have overdrawn the distinction between the East and the West and have been unfair to the large achievement of the Latin peoples. To such an indictment I can only repeat the plea made in the Introduction to the *Religion of Plato,* that I am by no means insensible to the grandeur of western Christianity, by the side of which the eastern Church, in its ages of decline after the fourth century, sinks into insignificance. But it remains true that in some important respects the Occident, in so far as it has been dominated by Roman legalism and medieval scholasticism, has added elements unfortunate in themselves and alien to the original spirit of the faith. From these religion, if it is to hold the modern mind, must be freed, and can most easily be freed by returning, for the moment at least, to the more Hellenic type of theology. We need to reintegrate for ourselves the Gospels and the philosophy of Plato, as this was once done in the dogma of Christ the Word.

To complete the series there is yet to be written, from the same point of view, a volume of essays dealing with such general topics as the difference between an authoritative and an absolute Church, the comparison of Christianity with its chief oriental rival, the rôle of mysticism, the interpretation of the creeds, and the sacramental office of the eucharist. Then to those readers who have kindly come with me so far, I may say:

> *Nos alia ex aliis in fata vocamur,*
> *Vobis parta quies.*

P. E. M.

Princeton, N. J.
April 10, 1927.

CONTENTS

	PREFACE	V
I	THE EARLY CHURCH	3
II	THE SETTING OF GNOSTICISM	30
III	THE CHRISTIAN THEOSOPHISTS	70
IV	THE SETTING OF HERESY	114
V	SABELLIANISM AND ARIANISM	139
VI	THE ARIAN SECTS	160
VII	ANTIOCH AND LAODICEA	184
VIII	THE CLIMAX OF HERESY	215
IX	CHALCEDON AND THE GREEK TRADITION	243
X	THE DOCTRINE OF THE LOGOS	277
XI	THE LOGOS (*continued*)	297
	APPENDIX A	331
	APPENDIX B	334
	APPENDIX C	339

CHRIST THE WORD

CHAPTER I

THE EARLY CHURCH

HOWEVER we interpret the personal claims attributed to Jesus, and whatever construction we put on the story of the Resurrection, one indisputable fact remains, that Christianity began with the belief in a superhuman founder. To the band of apostles and disciples gathered together in Jerusalem after the crucifixion, this Jesus whom they had accompanied in his mission through the lake towns and among the hills of Galilee, a friend quick to respond to all the compassions of humanity yet unyielding in principle and capable at times of scorching indignation, a teacher who arrogated to himself a sublime authority and whose words, marvellously simple and direct, seemed yet to elude them with mysterious hints of a new faith,—to these Christians, as they were soon to be named, their Master appeared in memory to have been a man like to them-

selves and at the same time something more
than man. Now at least, after his humiliation,
he had been raised up to stand at the right hand
of God as judge and Lord of the world; and in
recollection they saw the light of that deifica-
tion upon his face while he walked with them on
the earth. He was the Jesus whom they had
known, one person, whether in the flesh or in
glory; but his nature presented itself to them
in a double aspect, human and divine. This was
not a metaphysical theorem, not a doctrine
which they had reasoned out, but a conviction
born of experience.

That was the conclusion of our study of the
New Testament;[1] and that must be the introduction to our survey of the literature from
the Apostolic Fathers to the Council of Chalcedon, in which this same Jesus of Nazareth,
under the influence of the Greek tradition yet
without losing his original character, became
Christ the Word. In an earlier volume of the
series we have seen how for Plato the starting
point of the religious life was philosophy, where
he held that immediate truth could be attained,
and how from thence he developed a theology
and a mythology with diminishing claims to

[1] *The Christ of the New Testament*, 281f.

certitude.[2] Here we shall see religion traversing
the same line, but in the reverse direction. The
Christian began with a myth,[3] which he regarded as a demonstrable event of history,
while for him theology, as a system, and philosophy were true only in so far as they could be
made conformable to, and explanatory of, that
basis of his faith. The extraordinary thing we
shall have to note is that, despite the alien
source of the new myth, the theology and philosophy of the Greek Fathers should have
turned out in essential matters so thoroughly
Platonic, or, more accurately expressed, could
have been adopted from Plato with so few
modifications. Such a coalescence may lead us
to conjecture that the mythology which Plato
sought to substitute for the old tales of the gods
was not so much antagonistic to the faith of
Christianity as imperfectly Christian. And that
is indeed the case: the poetical flights of the
Phaedo and the *Republic* and the *Timaeus*
needed only to be stripped of their more fanciful elements to fall bodily into the Christian

2 *The Religion of Plato*, 17.
3 I must say here, what I have said before, that by the use of the
word "myth" nothing is implied prejudicial to the truth of the
event so designated. It simply means that any commingling of
the two spheres of the divine and the human, any revelation of
God to man, must assume an anthropomorphic character.

scheme, and these dialogues, especially the
Timaeus, were accepted by the liberal Fathers
as directly inspired by the Spirit of God or,
more naïvely, as plagiarisms from the books
of Moses. From hints here and there it could
even be surmised that Plato himself was dimly
aware of a theophany to come, of which his
allegories were a prophecy. Socrates in the
Apology had warned the Athenians of other
witnesses to the soul who should appear after
him and avenge his death; and elsewhere he had
admitted that, for all the reasoning and high
imaginings of philosophy, the full truth could
not be known until revealed to man by the
grace of God (*theia moira*). So in the parable
of the cave the seer who descended voluntarily
from the vision of light to bring salvation to
those in darkness was easily taken to be a type
of the Redeemer, as was also the portrait of the
suffering just man in the second book of the
Republic.

It is this fact, the Platonism of the philosophy finally developed by Christianity and the
semi-Christian nature of the mythology in
which at the last Plato clothed his philosophy,
it is this similarity of the ground traversed by
the two great spiritual movements of antiquity,

that justifies us in taking them together as a single body of religious experience. And it is this tradition, Platonic and Christian at the centre, this realization of an immaterial life, wrought into the very texture of the Greek language, that lies behind all our western culture. Without it, so far as I can see, we should have remained barbarians; and, losing it, we are in peril of sinking back into barbarism.[4] The task of the present day, as I see it, for those who would oppose the threatening tide of dissolution and materialism, is to sever from this tradition the ephemeral intrusions of superstition and metaphysics, and so to recapture the truth at the heart of it as a rallying point for the best thought of our time as it was for the best thought of the past.

To some critics it will appear—as I confess it seemed, or almost seemed, to myself at one time—that the first step in this purgation would be to go back to the method of philosophy, taking pure intuition as the starting point of religion, and allowing mythology to come in at the end as a more or less serious play of the imagination. Does it not for the modern mind, such critics would say, endanger the very possi-

4 *The Religion of Plato,* Preface, vii.

bility of religion to demand that its foundation shall be a belief in some supernatural event of long ago? And the implied answer is in harmony with the present wide-spread desire to obtain the benefits of faith through a sort of vague theism without any definite content of dogma. But I am sure that this would not have been the answer of Plato himself, could the question have been proposed to him in such a form. He would have felt that this myth of Christianity gave precisely the one thing, the *unum neces-sarium,* for which he had been searching all his life, and that the compulsion it had laid upon him was evidence of its veracity. He was ready, he says in that conversation which he imagines to have taken place between Socrates and the young Phaedrus on the banks of the Ilissus— he was ready, if he could find any man so much as able to discern "a One and Many in nature," to walk in his footsteps as though he were a god. Suppose it could have been told him that after six hundred years a student of his works would be applying these words to a person who did not discern, but in himself claimed to be, the One and the Many![5] Would not Plato have said, "My Lord and my God"?

5 Clem. Alex., *Strom.* II, xx, 104. For Plato's conception of such

At any rate there can be no doubt in regard to the position of the Christian missionaries. To them revelation by means of a mythical event was not a denial but a direct confirmation of philosophy; as, indeed, the possibility of such an event was implied in any satisfactory quest of the truth. "The maker and father of this universe," Plato had avowed in his old age, "is hard to discover, and, having found Him, one cannot declare Him to all men." It was almost a challenge to such an avowal, when St. Paul made his proud assertion on the Areopagus: "For as I passed by, and beheld your devotions, I found an altar with this inscription, TO THE UN-KNOWN GOD. Whom therefore ye ignorantly worship, him declare I unto you." And Justin Martyr, in a passage so notable as to warrant quotation at length, develops this idea and adroitly connects the statements of Plato and St. Paul:

"What we have surpasses all human doctrine by reason of the fact that the whole rational principle (*to logikon*) of the universe became for our sakes the manifest Christ, as body, reason (logos), and soul. All the fine sayings and discoveries of philosophers and lawgivers in

a realization of philosophy in the life of Socrates, see my *Platonism*, 303 (second edition).

the past were their elaborations as by search
and speculation they laid hold of fragments of
the logos. And because they did not know the
logos in all its parts as Christ, they often con-
tradicted themselves and one another. Even so,
those who before Christ undertook to speculate
upon these high things and to test them by the
human reason were carried off to trial in the
courts as impious and overcurious. Thus Socrates, who set out on this path most boldly of
them all, suffered the same charges as are laid
against us: for they said that he introduced
new daemonic powers and refused to accept the
gods of the city. But really, by ejecting Homer
and the other poets from his ideal State, he
taught men to renounce the evil daemons who
had behaved as the poets represented, and
urged them on to recognize through rational
inquiry the God unknown to them, saying: 'The
father and creator of all things is not easy to
discover, nor, having found him, can one safely
announce him to all men.' But this is precisely
what our Christ did through his power. For no
one ever was persuaded by Socrates to die for
this belief, whereas by Christ, the Christ known
also in part to Socrates (for he was and is the
logos in all men . . .), not philosophers and
scholars only have been so persuaded, but la-
bouring men and the very ignorant, even to
contempt of honour and fear and death. And
that because the doctrine of Christ is the power

of the ineffable Father and no artifice of human reasoning."[6]

I recall no other single passage in the Fathers which expresses so tersely and penetratingly the relation of Christianity to the Greek tradition, or could so well serve as a portal to all that will follow in this volume. It shows at once how religion had gained in efficacy by taking its initial stand on a mythological fact, and how the theoretical explanation of this fact had come to be clothed in language borrowed from philosophy.

On the theoretical side Justin, though he speaks as one of the Apologists, is in advance of his age. At the first, in those writers commonly grouped together as Apostolic, or Subapostolic,[7] there was little desire to connect the object of their worship with the conquests of pagan wisdom. Christ was primarily for them a beloved guide in the new way of purity and peace, as opposed to the old way of lust and distraction pursued by the heathen world. Religion was emphatically a life, not a speculation, and the Church was a small body of saints set apart from society to await the second coming

[6] *Apology*, II, x.
[7] For a chronological survey of the Greek Fathers see Appendix A.

of the Lord. In so far as they sought to account historically for their faith, they were content with what came to them from the Hebrew Bible. The revelation of the Word, with its miraculous power to convert the heart, was merely a more authoritative voice of the Spirit which under the old dispensation had spoken to and through Abraham and Moses and the prophets.

This is seen clearly in the earliest of the Fathers, Clement of Rome, who some time towards the end of the first century, probably before the composition of the fourth Gospel, wrote a letter of exhortation to the church at Corinth which had fallen into dissensions. The great words with Clement are humility and concord. "Let us put on the garment of concord in humility,"[8] he exclaims; and this is the constant burden of his appeal. Now the virtue inculcated by the Bishop of Rome is little more than another name for the "fear of God" that to the prophets and moralists of Israel was the beginning of wisdom and the means of salvation. It had a double source, on the one hand springing from the creature's sense of insignificance and impurity before the

---

[8] I, xxx, 3: Ἐνδυσώμεθα τὴν ὁμόνοιαν ταπεινοφρονοῦντες.

face of the tremendous and holy Jehovah, on the other hand, in its aspect of concord and of patience towards men, being an imitation of the long-suffering temper of God (*makrothymia*) under the provocations of human sin and rebellion and faithlessness.[9] Nor had the men of old, so commanded to fear and imitate God, been left without indications of His nature and work. Christ himself, the wisdom of God, the Word, the Holy Ghost, had conversed with them, though unknown, in his own voice and through the lips of those who without seeing yet believed. Only now for us, in the fulness of time, this same Spirit of God has appeared in the flesh, as man amongst men, and has proclaimed the truth in language which no one can misunderstand without sin.

The theophany is thus to Clement a natural consequence of prophecy; in it is contained the sum of faith and morality, and from it flow also the need of orderly worship, the sanctification of the Church as the body of the Lord, and the sacramental institution of the eucharist. But there is no attempt to develop a Christology or a theology from this starting point, no hint of the great mystery involved in the Incarnation,

9 *Ibid.*, I, xviii-xx.

viz. that by this gracious condescension what under the old dispensation was shown as the long-suffering of God has taken the form of humility, not to say humiliation, within the divine nature itself. There is even no true trinitarianism, though the three names occur in the doxologies of Clement, but a kind of monotheism which in some undefined manner embraces the Son, while the Holy Ghost is left in the penumbra of divinity as the spirit of God in Christ, or as Christ himself, or as "the faith and hope of the elect."[10]

Perhaps the sharpest formulation of this early belief was given by Ignatius, a somewhat later contemporary of Clement, in his letter to the Magnesians: "For the divine prophets lived according to Jesus Christ. Therefore they were persecuted, being inspired by his grace to convince unbelievers that there is one God, the God who manifested Himself through Jesus Christ His Son, who is His Word proceeding from silence."[11] This is the substance of the myth for which the world was waiting and philosophy

[10] *Ibid.*, I, lviii, 2.
[11] It is to be noted that this same Ignatius is an outspoken antagonist of any attempt to Judaize in the Church. So, in general, the early Fathers insist equally on the continuity of the faith and on the singularity of the new revelation.

was groping, and which was to supplant the intractable legends of Olympus and the extravagant theosophy of the Orient.

Above all it is the life of the little communities scattered along the routes of the Mediterranean that amazes the reader of history. Ignatius travels from Antioch to Rome and martyrdom under the guard of ten soldiers whom he calls leopards for their cruelty; and as he passes from one centre of faith to another the people, or their leaders, come out to greet him as though he were a crowned victor. A joyous spirit of fellowship binds these societies together, and church sends encouragement to church across the boundless sea of paganism. And of the divine source of this new concord the partakers were fully conscious, as can be seen in the so-called *Epistle to Diognetus,* which, though of somewhat later date, is commonly reckoned among the writings of the Apostolic Fathers. There we learn that the distinction between Christians and other men was held to consist neither in country nor in language. The faithful are found residing in Greek and barbarian cities, as it may be, and following the local customs in all the outer circumstances of life. Yet withal they display the wonderful and confessedly invidious character of a separate citizenship. They dwell in their own fatherlands, but as if sojourners only; they share all things as citizens, while suffering all things as aliens. They marry like other men, and bear children, but they do not expose their offspring. Their lot is cast in the flesh, but they do not live after the flesh. They obey the law, but they go beyond the requirements of the law in their own abstinence. To put it shortly, what the soul is to the body, that the Christians are in the world. For as the soul dwells in the body, yet is not of the body, so do Christians abide in the world, yet are not of the world. The flesh hates and wages war upon the soul, though it suffers no evil therefrom, because it is prevented from gratifying its lusts, and in like manner and for the same reason the world hates the Christians. And as the soul loves the flesh which hates it, so do Christians love those who persecute them. And as the soul dwells immortal in a mortal tabernacle, so do Christians sojourn among corruptible things, waiting for the incorruptibility which is in heaven. God has appointed them to this great post, and it is not for them to decline it.[12]

[12] *Epistle to Diognetus*, V, vi. I have drawn largely on the translation by Kirsopp Lake.

There is a striking difference between the tone of the canonical books of the New Testament and that of these documents of the so-called Apostolic age. One misses the note of direct authority; the writers are aware of their secondary position as maintainers merely of what has been given. Nor have they the intellectual qualities that appeal to us in some of the theologians of a later period; one feels that they are simple men preaching to a simple folk, without culture or worldly charm. Yet it would be a dull soul who could read these epistles without a thrill of elation. However clothed in humility, this new thing that has entered into the life of mankind appears in them with a marvellous freshness of beauty and with kindling power. After many excursions in the broad lands of Christian literature, one may come back to the untutored words of the Apostolic Fathers as perhaps the best witness to the mission of the Church as an organization. Here is life, and here in germ all that is needed of theology: belief in an all-creating bountiful God, who revealed His will through the prophets of old, and now by a special act of mercy has manifested Himself in His Son; belief in the Holy Ghost as the spirit of the Father and the Son

communing with the spirit of man; belief in
the divine law as exemplified in the character of
Jesus; in the hope of life and glory as secured
by the Resurrection; in the eucharist as the
mystical sign and instrument of the redemption of the flesh; in the Church as the body of
the Lord and a chosen people; in the bishops as
the appointed channel of sacramental grace
and as the authentic bearers of the tradition.
Vast treasures of philosophy are to be ex-
pended on the myth of the Incarnation as the
central fact of this faith; but nothing of essential importance will be added, while some of
the actual additions will have rather the nature
of intrusions from an alien world.

Meanwhile the Church is growing, and the
State is becoming uneasily aware of this *im-
perium in imperio*. It will endeavour to crush
its upstart rival by physical persecution and
moral defamation. As for the former means, it
is a common saying that the blood of the mar-
tyrs is the seed of the Church; but the historian,
looking more dispassionately on events, may
ask whether persecution would not have had
quite other effects if the early emperors had
proceeded to any such systematic measures as
were pursued by Diocletian and Maximin when

the enemy had grown too powerful to be suppressed, or whether even then the result would not have been extermination had the policy of these rulers not been suddenly, providentially some would say, stayed by political revolution. In fact however persecution, such as it was, did not suppress Christianity, though it left to the Church a heritage of difficulties in dealing with the lapsed which narrowly imperilled her unity.

As for the work of defamation, this in the main was childish and strangly ignorant; nor till later, when such defence was scarcely needed, did its refutation demand great intelligence on the part of the so-called Apologists. From the philosophical point of view the best works on the Christian side, barring always the *Contra Celsum* of Origen which belongs to another age, are the *Apology* of Justin and the *Supplication* of Athenagoras, and of these the latter is the more exemplary.

Athenagoras, supposed to be an Athenian convert from philosophy, addressed his treatise to the Emperors Marcus Aurelius and Commodus about the year 177. His plea in general is based on the principle of equity, that the Christians should not be condemned merely for their name, but should stand trial on their be-

liefs and conduct like any other men charged
with crime. With some inconsistency, perhaps,
he then proceeds to prove that the actual
charges brought against the Christian doctrine
and life are utterly false. These incriminations
touch the two aspects of religion: otherworldliness and morality,—under the former the indictment of atheism, under the second that of
Oedipean intercourse and Thyestean banquets.

The answer of Athenagoras to the charge of
atheism takes the form of a scathing counter-
attack on the follies of polytheism and idolatry
as practised by the accusers of Christianity,
and of arguments to show that, so far from
being atheists, the followers of Christ worship
the one God dimly divined by the wiser poets
and diligently sought by the great philosophers.
Again, as in Justin, the retort runs that the
deity whom Plato had found hard to discover
and impossible to declare to all men, this Father
and Maker of the world so passionately desired
yet still unknown to human wisdom, has revealed Himself clearly from old time through
the prophets. He whom the Christians adore is
the Lord of all, uncreated, eternal, invisible,
impassible, illimitable, encompassed by light
and beauty and spirit and power unspeakable;

together with the Son, who is the Logos of the
Father in idea and operation, by whom and
through whom were all things made, the Father
and the Son being one; and with them the Holy
Ghost, the prophetic spirit, which is an effluence of God, flowing from Him and returning
back to Him like a beam of the sun. And this
assertion of Christian otherworldiness is com-
pleted by affirming the Platonic distinction between matter and spirit, the creature and the
Creator, which, however, does not exclude faith
in the resurrection of the body. Curiously
enough, nothing is said of the Incarnation of
the Logos, probably from a cautious desire to
keep the argument as simple as possible, and to
avoid "topics irrelevant to the subject in hand."

The charges of immorality are rebutted negatively by calling for evidence, and positively
by showing how far the Christian ethics, based
on a pure theism and on the final accountability
of all men in the day of judgement, surpass the
highest reach of paganism. It is not strange, he
adds, that those who worship the Zeus of popular tradition should invent against the Christians
tales of promiscuous licence and Thyestean
cruelty. In fact, as we know from other sources,
there seems to have been a wide-spread belief

that the Christian agape, or eucharist, was celebrated by sacrificing and devouring an infant, and that at a certain moment the lights were quenched for the sake of wild and indiscriminate debauchery.[13] Rumours of a similar kind were promulgated by the orthodox against some of the baser of the gnostic sects. It is quite credible, considering the age, that such abominations were carried out here and there in the conventicles of those who called themselves by the name of Christ; but it was easy for Athenagoras to flout such accusations when brought against the body of the Church.

One wonders whether this powerful and really unanswerable apology ever reached the ears of the God-seeking and persecuting emperor to whom it was directed, and, if so, what impression it made on him.

We know nothing of the life of Athenagoras, or of the motives that drew him from philosophy to Christianity; but in the case of another of the Apologists, Justin, who suffered martyrdom in the year 165, we have a vivid account of the transaction from his own pen, true, one believes, in substance, though romantically

13 Justin Martyr, Theophilus, and Minucius Felix refer to the same stories.

coloured in details. The story is told in the introduction to his *Dialogue with the Jew Trypho*. He was, he says, walking one forenoon in the covered colonnade (probably of Ephesus), when he was accosted politely by Trypho and several others, out of respect for the philosopher's robe which he still wore though a Christian. Their conversation soon turned to the subject of philosophy, which the Jew avers he held in reverence because it discoursed of God and the providential government of the world. And Justin admits, paraphrasing a famous passage of Plato,[14] that philosophy is the noblest possession of man—or at least ought to be so, and would be so, had not those who made it their profession forgotten its high theme and fallen into sectarian disputations. This defalcation Justin has learned from his own sad experience, for he has passed through the schools and found them all wanting. First he had tried a Stoic; but had left him when it appeared that this professor of the Porch neither had any knowledge of God to impart nor thought such instruction essential.[15] Next he betook himself to a keen Peripatetic, but was

---

[14] *Timaeus*, 47B.
[15] This may sound strange of a Stoic, but it was precisely the doctrine of Aristo of Chios, a disciple of Zeno.

rebuffed by the man's evident worldliness. From the Aristotelian he went to a celebrated Pythagorean; but here again he got no satisfaction, for his new teacher required a long training in music and astronomy and geometry before he would approach the topic in which Justin was interested. God was very far from the Pythagorean's mind. And so, as a last resort, Justin applies to a Platonist. Here, surely, he should be directed to the way he was seeking; and to a certain stage he was not disappointed. He says of himself that he made marvellous progress day by day in wisdom, and that the opening to him of Plato's world of Ideas gave as it were wings to his soul; in a little while he thought he should veritably see God, for this is the purpose and goal of the Academic quest.

In this frame of mind, Justin continues, he went out one day to a place in the country not far from the sea, thinking there to find complete solitude and a quiet space for the celestial vision. To his surprise he saw himself followed by an old man of mild and venerable countenance, a Christian as it turned out, to whom Justin, on being questioned, makes profession of his philosophic creed.

" 'Does philosophy, then, confer happiness?'
said he, interrupting me.

" 'Assuredly,' said I, 'and it alone.'

" 'What then is philosophy?' he asked; 'and
what is the happiness it confers? Pray tell me, if
there be no objection.'

" 'Philosophy,' I replied, 'is knowledge of
that which really is, and perception of the truth;
happiness is the prize of this knowledge and
wisdom.'

" 'And what is it that you call God?' said he.

" 'That which remains ever the same, always
itself, and is the cause of being to all other
things, that is God.' So I answered him, and he
heard with pleasure."

From this definition they pass to a discussion
of the question whether the Platonic philosophy
really confers the boon it professes to offer.
Knowledge of God, the Christian demurs, is
different from that of the arts, and must come
by immediate intuition, not by practice and
training.—Justin admits this, but asserts that,
according to Plato, the high reason of man, the
nous, is in nature akin to God, and therefore
possesses the faculty of divine vision.—How
does it happen then, the Christian asks, that all
men do not enjoy this privilege, as they would
if it were merely a matter of the soul's kinship
with God.—Only the souls purged and purified

by virtue, Justin replies, can exercise the faculty; and even to these the vision is barely possible save at those times when, not yet involved in the obstructions of the flesh, they ranged aloft and came face to face with the object of their constant love.—But, retorts the Christian, we have no recollection of such adventures in a prenatal life, and therefore, on that ground, have no right to believe that we have seen, or ever shall see, God. Neither, indeed, have we any right to argue that the soul is immortal, against all the evidence of the senses. No, there is nothing for us but to abandon these guesses of the philosophers for the books of the seers to whom knowledge of God was given by inspiration, and whose prophetic claims have been confirmed by history. Pray you, then, that the gates of light may be opened to you; for these things cannot be perceived or grasped save by him to whom God and His Christ impart the gift of understanding.—And so, Justin says to his Hebrew interlocutors, by reflection on what I then heard a flame was kindled in my breast, and you see me now a philosopher indeed, but a Christian too; and I would have all men hearken, as I do, to the words of the Saviour.

The rest of the dialogue consists of a long-drawn appeal on the part of Justin to the Jewish scriptures, showing how everywhere they are filled with symbols and intimations and plainly uttered warnings of that great event in time when the eternal Son, the Logos, the celestial Reason, which gave to the world its mystery of ordered beauty and spoke of old to Israel by the voice of prophecy, should appear visibly amongst men as body and soul and spirit, and so should reveal once for all the will and being of God.

It seems to me evident, from hints here and there in other writings of the period, that the manner of Justin's conversion, though the particular incidents related by him may be fiction, was typical of the experience which was drawing the better minds into the Church. How many thoughtful men at that time were studying the philosophers of the past and testing the various schools of the present in the hope of discovering a warrant for their faith which the traditional mythology could not give them, or gave them only by violent distortions of allegory! And something solid and secure they did find, those of them at least who took the right way. In the Ideal doctrine of Plato there had been added to philosophy a conception of the otherworld stimulating at once to the imagination and the emotions, a conception providing a sound basis for morals and to the finer minds opening a door of refuge from an actual world that appeared to be sinking into the illusions of troubled slumber. The Christians themselves were not slow to recognize this gain, as may be seen by the generous admission of Justin[16] and as becomes clearer in the later adaptation of Platonic imagery to the vision of the Kingdom of Heaven. But this alone was not enough for the religious craving of that age, or of any age. He who penetrated into the sphere of Ideas might be likened to the prince of our fairy tale who strayed into the enchanted grove and palace of the sleeping beauty, where all about him was a scene marvellously rich and peaceful, but a silence also and an emptiness as of death.

I do not mean to say that the Ideal world to Plato himself, or to such a pupil of the Academy as Plutarch, held no living God—far from that. Nevertheless it is true that the deity of Plato's religion was too much an inference of the reason, too remote from humanity, and that Plutarch's deity was too deeply involved in the

16 So his famous saying: Οὐκ ἀλλότριά ἐστι τὰ Πλάτωνος δόγματα τοῦ Χριστοῦ.

mists of daemonism, to satisfy the hearts of men yearning for spiritual compassion and divine fellowship. And all about this brave effort of philosophy lay the irredeemable mass of Hellenistic superstition. Something still was wanted, a voice that should have the authority of revelation from above rather than the plausibility of persuasion from below.[17] It was necessary to make a fresh start, and so to rebuild the fabric of religion on the foundation of a myth capable of compelling belief by its own aspect of truth, and capable also of assimilating the veritable conquests of philosophy. When then the searchers of that age read in the fourth Gospel that the Word became flesh, it seemed to them as if, by a sudden burst of light from on high, all the difficulties and obscurities of Plato's effort to explain the immanence of Ideas in terrestrial phenomena were lifted, while to the realm of pure Ideas came life and hospitality by the presence of a God visible there to the eye of faith, as the Lord was once seen and heard by Adam walking in the garden in the cool of the day.

---

[17] *Epistle to Diognetus*, viii, 1: Τίς γὰρ ὅλως ἀνθρώπων ἠπίστατο τί ποτ' ἐστὶ θεός, πρὶν αὐτὸν ἐλθεῖν;

CHAPTER II

THE SETTING OF GNOSTICISM

THE course of the Church was determined by three great contentions—with pure paganism, with Gnosticism, and with heresy in its own body—which imposed their mark also on the three periods of patristic literature after the canonical and Apostolic writers. As for the first of these conflicts, we have seen how the Apologists scorned their spiritual detractors and sought to placate their physical persecutors in the pagan world. The battle indeed did not end with them; but in principle the victory was won by Justin and Athenagoras, and from that time the better minds turned in ever increasing numbers away from heathendom.

Meanwhile a foe of a different stripe was gathering energy, more dangerous than the avowed enemy for the reason that it professed to be more Christian than the Church, while bringing to religion a treasure of insight gar-

nered from all corners of the known earth. This
was Gnosticism, a strange medley of follies and
sublimities, a many-headed monster, whose
origin has been a puzzle to scholars, and whose
fascination is still felt in the most unexpected
places. To understand the situation at all one
must have in mind the two main currents cir-
cling through the religious atmosphere of the
day, or, if you will, the two rocks of Scylla and
Charybdis between which the Church had to
steer its perilous course. These were, in a word,
metaphysics and superstition.

The metaphysical current sweeping over the
second century, the flowering time of the Gnostics, was nothing new in history, nor did it cease
with that epoch. It is simply the very human
temptation to subject the total impression of
the universe to some formula of the reason or
the imagination which will reconcile all the perplexing contradictions of reality in an ultimate
unity. We see this process at work in the earliest philosophers of Ionia, who postulated a
single self-evolving substance, whether water
or air or fire, behind the variegated phenomena
of the earth. It begins to reach out into the religious field among the so-called *theologoi*.

"Listen not to me but to the logos," says Heraclitus, "and admit the wisdom of the maxim, All things are one." The same belief, in about the same words, was common to Xenophanes and the Eleatic school; and it is sung by Aeschylus:

> Zeus is the air and earth, and Zeus the sky;
> All things are Zeus, and what beyond may lie.

It dominated the later mystery-mongers (and from them gets into St. Paul) in some such form as this: "One is the all, and through it the all, and to it the all."[1]

For the most part this is the innocent play of the imagination; and its characteristic note is the sort of pantheism echoes of which may be heard the world over, sometimes modulated to music of exquisite beauty, as in such outflowings of romance as inspired Wordsworth's *Tintern Abbey*—and there it might be allowed to remain, floating in the vague of sentimental revery. The more specifically rationalistic treatment of the impulse took its rise in Greece with Aristotle; and the direction here is rather towards a harsh transcendence than towards a fanciful immanence. From Aristotle to Ploti-

[1] For other examples of this tendency see Norden, *Agnostos Theos*, 240 ff.

nus the way of the transcendental reason runs in a straight line.[2]

Reason in its progress towards a transcendental monism and the imagination in its progress towards a pantheistic monism may seem to be moving along divergent routes, but the difference is only apparent; their starting point is the same desire to escape the limitations of experience, and in the end they lose their identity in an indistinguishable abstraction. So at the close of our period we find the two ultimates of pantheism and transcendentalism wedded together in the mystical rhapsody of the pseudo-Dionysius, where the mind jumps from the "positive way" of regarding God as the sum of all Being to the "negative way" of regarding Him as pure Non-Being, or *vice versa* from absolute isolation above the world to absolute confluence with the world, and back again, with

[2] In holding Aristotle responsible for the invasion of rationalism into Hellenistic thought I do not forget the sounder elements of his philosophy, nor am I unaware that my treatment of this great name, owing to the limitations of my theme, is open to the charge of onesidedness. But it is a fact that Aristotle, by absorbing both the God and Ideas of Plato's later theology into his earlier conception of the Good (*Republic,* vi), and then raising the Good into an absolute *telos* as the Unmoved Mover, did prepare the way for transcendental monism (see *Hellenistic Philosophies,* 206 ff.). Unfortunately in the period we are considering it was this special aspect of Aristotle's philosophy which combined with other currents of metaphysical rationalism to influence the course of religion.

no appreciation of its own acrobatic agility in these dizzy heights—

Pinnacled dim in the intense inane.

And, indeed, when once you have overleapt the barriers of common sense it makes little difference in which direction you turn, and whether at the last you say that God is all or that God is nothing. Against the debauch of reason the restraining modesty of dualism was preserved for pagan philosophy and handed on by such notable Platonists as Maximus of Tyre and Plutarch and Atticus. But outside of Christianity the genuine followers of Plato in this respect were not many; the very atmosphere breathed by the theosophists of the second century might be said to be impregnated with the metaphysical virus.

As for the superstition of the age, one hardly knows where to begin or how to select an illustration, so thick and dense and manifold was the stream of grotesque myths and morbid fears flowing over the lands, like vapours drifting from the decay of dead religions. Read of them in Lucian's satires, or take up Cumont's popular manuals or any of the treatises dealing with the practices of magic,—it is as though, coming to them from Christianity, one were plunged

into a backwash of foul waters. For our purpose
the most significant of these superstitions, the
one which most influenced the early Gnostics,
against which the Christian theologians, beginning with St. Paul, protested most frequently,
and which yet has persisted among large circles
of the ignorant down to the present day, was
the belief in astrology. The scourge seems to
have had its source in Babylonia, though probably from a cult much modified by the Persian
domination. In essence it taught that this
earth and our human souls are under the control of the seven planets, or the daemons who
have their seat in the planets; and as these
lords are of a more or less malignant nature, the
prime office of religion is to divulge some magical formula which will set the initiate free from
their oppressive tyranny. These were the prin-
cipalities and powers which Paul defied as unable to separate us from the love of God in
Christ Jesus.

For the earthly span of man's life the way of
escape from these sidereal lords, or, if not escape, the means of adjusting one's course to
their fatality, was through the knowledge of
their operation obtained by casting horoscopes;
and there is evidence that this practice was

wide-spread from the palace to the hovel. The
system in vogue seems to have corresponded
substantially with that employed in the Middle
Ages, and may still be found in popular manuals and almanacs.[3] One special difficulty, however, which the ancients encountered and of
which the critics of astrology made much, was
caused by the lack of time-pieces for register-
ing the exact moment of birth, and of ephemer-
ides for ascertaining the exact position of the
stars; since the art of celestial divination depends on absolute precision in these matters.
The fact, for example, whether Jupiter is just
below or just above the eastern horizon when
the horoscope is cast may determine the predic-
tion of an infant's career as monarch or clown.
In his *Refutation* Hippolytus, who traces all
religious aberrations back to Babylon, gives an
amusing account of one of the methods adopted
to obviate this difficulty. An attendant sits by
the bed of the woman in travail, and at the instant of parturition makes a signal by striking

[3] By the precession of the equinoxes the constellations which
gave their names to the twelve signs of the Zodiac have advanced
nearly 30° since the rules of astrology were laid down, while
the signs have retained their old names. Thus the constellation
Aries is now in the sign Taurus. It is a curious fact that modern
astrologers take account of the signs, not of the constellations,
and calculate the effect, *e.g.* of the sign Taurus as if the Bull
were present in it.

a metallic gong; and warned by this sound the Chaldean, who from an elevated situation is contemplating the heavens, notes the rising zodiacal sign and so constructs his figures. Whereupon Hippolytus proceeds to show the fallacy of the system by proving that parturition is not an instantaneous event, and that, further, an indefinite interval of time elapses before the sound of the gong reaches the observer.[4]

For deliverance of the soul after death from the dominion of the planetary despots, knowledge was still the means, but of a different sort. To this end the great art was to be instructed in the names of the rulers, such *gnôsis* carrying with it, as commonly in magic, an ascendency over the possessor of the name.[5] As a theme of poetry the superstition of the age reached here perhaps its highest point; particularly in the Manichean sect the picture of the soul in its triumphant flight through the seven hostile spheres up to reunion with the super-celestial divinity has elements of epic sublimity. But on the other hand this same notion of power obtained by mere utterance of "the name" is the

[4] *Refutation*, IV, iv.
[5] The "name" among the Greeks and Hebrews, and generally in the ancient world, was the nearest equivalent linguistically to what we mean by "person" or "personality." So to take the name of God in vain was to offer insult to his person.

source of the most grovelling forms of incan-
tation.

These two currents, a speculative rationalism
that satisfies the demand for unity by the conception of an Absolute utterly severed from the
realm of mutability, and a superstition sinking
down into the grossest belief in magic and
daemonism, run all through the non-Christian
literature. There is something to astonish in the
mere contemporaneity of tendencies so diamet-
rically opposed to each other; but astonishment
may give way to bewilderment when we see
them, as they often were, inextricably inter-
knitted. The most rarefied metaphysics and the
most abject credulity would seem to be incompatible states of mind, yet a characteristic feature of the Hellenistic world is precisely the
coalescence of these contradictories. The point
of contact and fusion, I think, must be looked
for in the theory of intermediaries. Just so sure
as reason is allowed to play her game unchecked,
and thus, in contempt of life and experience, to
conceive ultimate reality as an abstraction out
of touch with all we know as real, just so certainly will the mind, appalled at the chasm left
between the abstract and the concrete, set to
work to bridge the gulf by the invention of an

ever increasing number of intermediaries; and on these intermediaries the mythopoeic faculty will lay hold with an audacity the more licentious because the restrictions of common sense have been ruled out from the beginning. Nature will have her revenge—*tamen usque recurret.*

A notable example of this law may be found in the metaphysical movement which attained its apogee in Plotinus. Here we see the Absolute placed high in a region beyond being and intelligence, isolated from life by reaches of ineffable vacuity. Yet this Absolute, as the final reality, must be the source of all that is real; and thus the void between the One that is above being and the absolute Multiplicity that is below being, the abyss of being between the two non-beings, is filled in with a series of intermediaries proceeding from the One by way of successive emanations which yet leave their source undiminished, unchanged, and unconcerned. Plotinus himself remains snugly within the safety of pure abstractions; but by the inevitable law of reaction the Neoplatonists who follow him as masters of the school take advantage of these intermediaries to introduce a host of daemons from the popular superstition and to debase their cosmic philosophy with magic ceremonies. History shows the break-down of metaphysics among the mystery-mongers who swarmed about the court of Julian the Apostate.

A similar and striking illustration of the natural course of metaphysics may be studied in one of the by-products of Judaism. Philo, distinguished as "the Jew," was born in Alexandria sometime in the second decade before Christ. He belonged to an important family of the Diaspora, *i.e.* of Israel scattered over the Mediterranean lands outside of Palestine. From the New Testament these Jews of the Dispersion are chiefly known to us for their proselytizing zeal; and it was primarily to the gentile hangers-on or semi-converts of their isolated synagogues that the early Christian missionaries made appeal. But if these exiles from Palestine were the means of spreading the Jewish monotheism over the world, they were also peculiarly open to influence from pagan philosophy; and of this ambiguous position Philo is a notorious example. He was, like St. Paul, a Hebrew of the Hebrews, fully convinced that his people were the appointed custodians of the very oracles of God. Yet at the same time he read the Scriptures with a brain

steeped in Greek philosophy; and he interpreted them accordingly, nursing his patriotism
the while on the pleasant illusion that whatever
of truth spoke from pagan literature had been
purloined out of the books of Moses. His life-
long task was to demonstrate how what he regarded as Platonism lay concealed allegorically
in the Pentateuch; so that in Jerome's day the
saying was current that either Plato Philonizes
or Philo Platonizes. But, as with the Aristotelianism of the age, the Platonism he had imbibed
came from a stream much muddied in its long
course and diverted into strange channels.

For some time there had been a tendency
among the reflective Jews to elevate the Jehovah of tradition, certainly in His origin a very
human and even passionate deity, into a region
far above contact with the compromising affairs
of life. His name was so awful that it could not
without desecration pass through the lips of
mortal man. The tetragrammaton (*i.e.* the
quaternion of consonants JHVH) could be
uttered only with vowels borrowed from another word; or for the proper name was sub-
stituted bodily some such term as "Place" or
"Height" or "Heavens." So thoroughly was
this prohibition carried out that to the present

day the correct vocalization of what the Authorized translators, following the Jewish custom, wrote as JeHoVaH and modern pedants write as JaHVeH remains a matter of doubt.[6] In part this process of sublimation was purely religious, instigated by reverence for the transcendent and ineffable holiness of the divine nature. But in the case of Philo we see also a deliberate effort to reinterpret the theology of Moses in terms of the regnant metaphysics; and it is not too much to say that this *mésalliance* of Jehovah with the Absolute of the schools was the chief cause of embarrassments from which religion has never yet shaken itself free. "The sum of the matter," says Philo, "is in the inspired oracles (the Bible), that 'God is not as man'; but neither is He as the heavens or the world. For these things are qualified forms and perceptible to the senses, whereas God is not even comprehensible to the intellect, except in His being; what we comprehend of Him is His existence, and besides bare existence nothing."[7]

[6] The grotesque form Jahveh, or Jahweh, has not even the excuse of being probably correct etymologically; yet it has fastened itself upon us. If pedantry of this sort were only suicidal it would be comparatively harmless, but it has the self-perpetuating power of malignant germs.

[7] *Quod Deus Im.*, 62.

And so, having refined the Jehovah of the Law and the prophets out of all contact with finite reality, Philo is confronted with the problem of reuniting this bloodless Absolute with the world as creator and providential ruler. To this end he follows the beaten track, thinking, like hundreds before and after him, to heal the breach by the aid of intermediaries, and borrowing these from whatever source lay open to him with not much care for their incompatibility one with another. As an avowed Platonist he will grasp at the mythology of the *Timaeus*: for, he says, God, perceiving that any fashioned work must be made in imitation of a pattern, and wishing to create this world after the fairest model, first formed a world of incorporeal Ideas as the archetype of that which was to be visible and corporeal.[8] Philo does not see that by depriving the pattern of its eternal independence by the side of God and altering it to a creation of God he has introduced a conception totally disruptive of the Platonic myth, and so goes on serenely to divest Ideas of all significance by describing them as a birth within the mind of the Creator, corresponding to the

[8] *De Op. Mundi,* 16. Characteristically Philo traces this supposed Platonic theory back to Moses.

design conceived in the brain of an architect before he begins to build.[9]

But to give to Ideas the rôle of a true intermediary still another step must be taken: they must be regarded as thoughts of the creative mind, yet as going forth also with delegated authority, like semi-individualized agents between God and His work. Thus they become the Powers. And then, lengthening the chain, Philo will separate the Powers from the Ideas as the active from the passive instrument of creation, and relegate the latter to a still lower rank in the scale. The order is no longer God and Power *or* Ideas, but God and Powers *and* Ideas. "For," as he now observes, "by these Powers was produced the incorporeal and intelligible world, the archetype of this phenomenal world, composed of invisible Ideas as this is composed of visible bodies."[10]

At this point the juncture of Philo's Hellenism with his Jewish inheritance becomes clear. These Powers, for all their Platonic and Stoic

[9] *Ibid.*, 24. This translation of Plato's Ideas from an eternal objective reality to subjective ideas within the mind of God, whoever is ultimately responsible for it, is one of the most momentous revolutions in philosophy. It is taken over by Plotinus and the Neoplatonists; it becomes in Christian theology a source of endless controversy.
[10] *De Conf. Ling.*, 172.

colouring, are identified by him with the Spirit (*ruach*) or the Angels of Jehovah, who appear often in the Old Testament as the means by which God makes His will felt in the world and in the hearts of men. And these Ideas are substitutes for the eternal "counsel of the Lord"[11] by which He works out His providential government. Powers and Ideas together are but "the spirit of the Lord, the spirit of counsel and might."

At the last all these symbols—Ideas, Powers, Spirit, Angels, Counsel—converge in the Logos. And, again, the terminology of Philo is of mixed origin, deftly, though no doubt innocently, chosen to disguise at once the ambiguity and the revolutionary character of his thought, which are the despair of his critics. On the one side the term logos came to him freighted with meaning from its use by a long succession of philosophers, with whom it signifies the *nous,* or "intelligence," immanent in the world, the inner force whereby the manifold phenomena of existence evolve in orderly sequence to form a cosmos. On the other side logos had already been adopted as a synonym for the counsel of

11 The *Sodh* or *'Etsath Jehovah,* as, *e.g.* Jer. xxiii, 18; Ps. xxxiii, 11; Isa. xi, 2.

the Lord by certain Hellenizing theologians of
Israel who not long before Philo's day had
composed those works of the so-called "Wisdom literature" now found in the Apocrypha
of the Old Testament. In the further process of
amalgamation Philo was assisted by the double
sense of the Greek term not apparent in its
English equivalent "word." For logos means
both a thought within the mind and the utterance of a thought in language, or, as the Stoics
were fond of distinguishing, it may be either
endiathetos or *prophorikos.* Now in the former
sense (*endiathetos*) logos readily becomes for
Philo a convenient name for the Ideal world
regarded as the thought or plan in the mind of
the Creator when He begins the task of creation,[12] and then, with equal convenience, for the
image of God, His seal imprinted on the objects of His handiwork, and so, in a manner
half Stoic, immanent in those objects.[13]

From this to the theological use of the logos
prophorikos (uttered) to denote the Word
going forth from God as his breath, or spirit,
and acting as a true intermediary, the transition is easy. The first step indeed had already

12 *De Op. Mundi,* 24, 25.
13 *De Fuga,* 12.

been taken in the Wisdom literature, where we read that "she is the breath of the power of God, and a pure influence flowing from the glory of the Almighty," and where, again, this "Wisdom that sitteth by the Throne" is identified with the Word by which all things were made. Nor were analogies lacking in the native tongue of Israel. From such passages as that in Genesis where the fact of creation follows the mere *fiat* of the Creator ("and God *said,*" *âmar*), the Rabbinical school had developed a theory of the *Memra* (Word, from the root *âmar*) as a power issuing from the mouth of God and manifesting itself almost, if never quite, as an independent mythological entity. Whether this use of *Memra* follows or precedes Philo in time, may be a question; in either case it shows the way taken by him in adapting the ancient theology of his people to the new current of metaphysics. He has to go only a little further and Logos becomes a common name for the two frankly intermediary Powers that accomplish the will of God: the divine Goodness by which the world is created, and the divine Authority by which the world is governed, the twain being symbolized separately by the Cherubim stationed before the

gate of Paradise or together by the flaming
sword.[14]

Evidently, to anticipate somewhat on our
theme, we are moving here in a field of ideas
curiously resembling the prologue to the fourth
Gospel, and it is even possible that the terminology of the evangelist was directly inspired by
the Philonic usage. But it is equally clear that
the identification of the Logos with a person
who, whatever his transcendental origin, appeared in the flesh and was known as a man
among men, gave this philosophy an entirely
new turn. It is true that Philo falls into the
language of personification. So, for instance,
he quite naturally compares the Logos, who
wears for vesture the visible web of phenomena,
with the High Priest, on whose robe the whole
world is represented in symbols, and adds: "His
(the Logos') father is God, the father of the
universe; his mother is the Wisdom of whom
all things have come into existence." And elsewhere, borrowing his terms from the same Wisdom literature, he speaks of the Logos as the
first-born son of God.[15] But this is no more than
the ambiguous figure of speech, common to

14 *De Cherubim,* 27 f.
15 *De Fuga,* 109; *De Vita Mosis,* ii, 117 ff; *De Agricultura,* 51,
et al.

poets and philosophers everywhere; the Logos
is personified, it is never a person. Such an ambiguity, indeed, adheres to the very notion of
an intermediary which, to fulfil its function,
must be defined now as an independent hypostasis and now as a mere attribute of the Omnipotent. Philo, as Zeller has well said, "combines both definitions without observing their
contradiction, nay he is unable to observe it, because otherwise the intermediary rôle assigned
to the divine Powers would be forfeited, even
that double nature by virtue of which they are
to be on the one hand identified with God, in
order that a participation in the Deity may by
their means be possible to the finite, and on the
other hand different from Him, in order that
the Deity, notwithstanding this participation,
may remain apart from all contact with the
world."[16] Now this "double nature" might seem
to bring the metaphysical conception of an intermediary and the Christian dogma of a mediator close together; but in fact they are radically distinct. Practically considered, a person
who mediates between two natures by embracing both is very different from an impersonal

[16] *Phil. der Griechen,* III, ii, 365, quoted by Schürer, *The Jewish
People,* V, 372.

intermediary which hovers indefinitely between
two natures and so really represents neither;
and, theoretically considered, the frank dualism
of Christianity, though it may be paradoxical
and difficult, does at least avoid the treachery of
a dualism which tries to swallow itself out of
sight. All this is implied in that revolutionary
sentence of the fourth Gospel: "And the Word
was made flesh."

Of the more debased forms of superstition
common to the age Philo, owing to his loyalty
to the Hebrew tradition, was happily free. So
far as he fails in this direction his error springs
rather from an exaggerated belief in the literal
inspiration of the so-called books of Moses, together with a desire to discover in them the
source of whatever is acceptable in Greek philosophy. As a result he is impelled to overlay the
plain narrative of Scripture with extravagant
allegories, which, if not superstition, are at the
best a kind of transcendental credulity. Thus,
to take a single illustration, the two accounts of
the creation of man in the first and second chapters of Genesis are supposed by him to anticipate the Platonic dualism—fantastically trans-
mogrified—of an Ideal man made in the image
of God as pure intelligence without body or sex,

and a material man fashioned of the dust of the ground.[17] This is innocent enough. But in the Cabbala, which had its commencement in the rabbinical school of Philo's time and reached its climax in the thirteenth-century compilation of the *Zohar*, the Jehovah of Genesis, under this same mania of metaphysics, evaporates into the En-Soph, the infinite conceived as Not-Being, while the Word, or *Memra*, by which He creates heaven and earth, is drawn out into ten intermediaries named Sephiroth, and is involved in about the wildest nonsense ever begotten in the superstitious brain of man.[18]

This invasion of credulity into a metaphysic mitigated by intermediaries would seem to be universal, rooted in human psychology. You will find it in India; it gave life to the hagiolatry of the Middle Ages; it is a notable mark of the romantic movement of which we are draining the lees; it played havoc with the ancient science of astronomy and threatens to overlay the abstractions of modern physics; it was, as we have seen, rampant in religion at the time when Gnosticism reared its head as the great rival of the Church.

[17] *Legum Alleg.*, i, 31 ff.
[18] Vulliaud, *La Kabbale juive*, I, 382 *et passim*.

Now the source and classification of the various gnostic sects which flourished in the second and third centuries offer one of the most vexed problems of scholarship. And, fortunately for me, it is not my business to write a history of this complicated movement, but merely to bring out its relation to Christianity:—

> Ye Powers
> And Spirits of this nethermost abyss,
> Chaos and ancient Night, I come no spy,
> With purpose to explore or to disturb
> The secrets of your realm, but by constraint
> Wand'ring this darksome desert, as my way
> Lies through your spacious empire up to light.[19]

The birth of what is properly called Gnosticism, if it had any single source, may with some plausibility be found in the imposition of the Zoroastrian religion of Ormazd and Ahriman on the astrological science of Babylon. Into this combination would then enter the Syrian belief in the Great Mother, fragments of the Jewish Law and story of creation, confused memories of Platonism and Pythagoreanism, and other myths and mysteries from Egypt and the far corners of the earth that were blowing over the Mediterranean world like chaff in a windstorm. Mingle these in varying proportions, and then

[19] *Paradise Lost,* ii, 968 ff.

add elements stolen from the Christian scheme of salvation and distorted so as to blend into the pagan background, and you have what is probably the most extraordinary example of religious syncretism in the whole range of history. Gnosticism was not a simple phenomenon, but resembled the polycephalic monster of Plato, with its ring of heads of all manner of beasts, tame and wild, which it was able to generate and metamorphose at will.[20]

In this shifting medley there are, however, two or three factors so constant as to lend a common character to the movement and to distinguish it from the parallel course of Christianity. Perhaps the most significant feature is the peculiar kind of dualism that runs through all the gnostic sects. Originally this dualism would seem to be connected with the Persian myth of the two hostile kingdoms of light and darkness and with the Assyrian conflict of Marduk and Tiâmat; but it was modified by the Hellenistic contrast of spirit and matter which points back to the Orphic mythology, and was deepened and blackened by the despondent outlook on life which was gradually eating its way to the heart of pagan society. The result, though

[20] *Republic*, 588c.

it carries with it some of the ideas of the *Phaed-rus* and the *Timaeus,* is radically different from the Platonic dualism. To Plato evil was inherent in the phenomenal world as the dark residuum of Necessity, the blank resistance to purpose which lurks unaccountably in nature and in the breast of man; but creation itself was the work of a God who in His goodness designs a cosmos that shall be so far as possible like Himself, good. To the Gnostic, on the contrary, the whole realm of creation was in origin and essence evil, and whatever stray elements of goodness may be discovered here are accidental, ravished, so to speak, from the region of light and against their will imprisoned in the mass of darkness. Even Plotinus and the Neoplatonists, much as they had in common with the Gnostics, repudiated vehemently this slanderous pessimism, while to the Christian idea of creation and the Fall it was totally abhorrent.

It will be seen at a glance how readily the prevalent tendencies of the age—the metaphysical absolute, intermediaries, and superstition—fitted into this frame of pessimism. The gnostic deity is raised into the region of pure abstraction, above any possible contact with the gross world of phenomena; he is unknown and unknowable in the fullest sense of the word, "the Abyss," "the Silence," "the God who is not," a stark negation of the reason set free from the trammels of experience. Then follows the inevitable revulsion, and between this inane abstraction and the realities of life there creeps in a hierarchy of intermediaries, growing ever longer and more complicated as sect treads upon the heels of sect. Under the influence of Babylonia and Syria these intermediaries would assume the form of the seven planetary spheres and their daemonic lords; in the West, pursuing the course which culminated in Neoplatonism, they lost their astrological character and became rather emanations from the absolute One, extending down from him, or it layer by layer, and composing with him the divine Pleroma. But whatever their names or disguises and however intricate their relation one with another, they are everywhere the offspring of the same metaphysical necessity, and everywhere they are associated with the superstitions of a moribund mythology. Somewhere in this scale of intermediaries the accident or crime of creation is inserted. The nature of the event varies with the mythological affiliations of the various sects, but in one thing

all the accounts agree: the existence of the phenomenal world is never, as in Platonism or
Christianity, dependent on the will of the supreme deity, but is referred to the weakness or
ignorance of some lower power, if not to his
downright malice; it is never a work of benefi-
cence to be purged of necessary imperfections
or restored to its pristine design, but is always
an alien intrusion, incapable of emendation and
calling for demolition. And here is the point of
juncture with the Old Testament. Jehovah to
the Jews was essentially the Creator, the Demiurge, He who evoked the world into being and
governs it to His own glory; to the Gnostic
such a deity cannot be supreme, he must be
ranked among the intermediaries and his work
must be degraded to a product either of mistaken zeal or of open maleficence. Hence the
Pentateuch, with its account of creation and its
imposition of the Law, is interpreted as an
apology inspired by Jehovah for his own glorification and at the expense of the true God; it
is to be accepted with condescending discrimination or rejected with indignant contempt.

The same harsh dualism, quite different from
that of Platonism and Christianity, determines
the gnostic theories of human life and morality.

In some way—each sect has its own myth—a
portion of the divine spirit akin to the supreme
God has been imprisoned in the created world,
and yearns for deliverance. This spark of the
divine is particularly lively in man, or in some
men, and constitutes the human spirit as distinct from the body and soul. Good and evil
thus cease to be the right and wrong use of the
will, or the upward and downward motion of
the soul as a unit, and become respectively the
properties of two mechanically associated elements or natures. Actions are good that help to
set the spirit free by breaking the bonds of this
unholy union, and the common precept of morality is: Abuse the flesh. As a result the ethics of
Gnosticism fall either into an exaggerated asceticism or into gross licentiousness. In the one
case the flesh is abused by denying all its natural wants; in the other case it may be abused
by regarding it as so foreign to the spirit that
no amount of physical indulgence will have any
deteriorating effect on the spiritual life but will
rather widen the gap between spirit and matter.
This latter form of inverted ethics was developed among the extremists who placed Jehovah
at the bottom of the scale of intermediaries, and
held that his Law should be disobeyed out of re-

gard to our kinship with the true God; morality
with these rebellious souls assumed the pleasant
and facile duty of doing everything forbidden
in the Ten Commandments! Such antinomians
no doubt were the exception, whereas asceticism would appear to have been the common
rule of life among the Gnostics; but any one
familiar with the ways of superstition and of
human nature will be slow to reject as slander
the hideous stories of debauchery told by Christian writers, notably by Epiphanius, against
certain of the sects.

It may well be asked what place could be
found in this conglomeration of moribund
pagan myths for Jesus of Nazareth, and, properly speaking, the answer would be none at all.
But the notion of a deity who somehow, with or
without his own volition, became entangled in
the corrupt mass of the world, or by his death
and dismemberment was the source of creation,
and who by his victorious escape or resuscitation
became a symbol or cause of human redemption,
was wide-spread; and one can see how, under
the impulse of indiscriminate syncretism, such a
legend might be transformed so as to include
some elements of the Christian soteriology.
After all, it is one of the strong arguments for

the authenticity of the new faith that it responded to a universal cry of the human heart for redemption; and we can understand, from the other side, how the better Gnostics would be impressed by the hope and sanctity of the followers of Christ, and would be sincere in their desire to appropriate from the Christian scheme of salvation whatever was available for their own cosmological system. Here the Joannine doctrine of the Word would come handy to their purpose, especially in those sects where the intermediaries were regarded as emanations from the Absolute. From the supreme God they imagined that there came forth a spiritual power, the Logos or Christos, which descended to earth, and by its presence helped the kindred spirit in mankind to break from the fetters of the body. It sounds very orthodox, but in fact offered no more than a parody of the true Incarnation. With their pessimistic scorn of the material world the Gnostics could not admit, in any literal sense, that the Word became flesh, nor with the mechanical dualism of their psychology could they accept the dogma of a Saviour who combined the complete human nature with his divine nature in a single personality. Hence they were driven to one or another

form of docetism. The Logos did not actually
partake of human life, but merely took up its
abode for a time in a certain man named Jesus;
it did not suffer on the Cross, but only seemed
to do so, while the real sufferer was the man
Jesus, from whom it departed at the moment of
death. Nor on the other hand was there any
genuine reconciliation of fallen human nature,
but only a temporary and seeming (docetic)
union of the two natures for the purpose of
winnowing out the spiritual from the non-
spiritual and psychic. The end was not a consummation or restoration of the creative act,
but a reversal of that act.[21]

A summary of the common features of so
heterogeneous a movement must necessarily be
vague, and to lend concreteness to the picture
it may be worth while to sketch briefly the best

[21] In essence docetism is an attempt to sublimate the Incarnation from an historical event into a purely abstract thesis of
philosophy, or for the theanthropic Jèsus of the Gospels to substitute a vague conception of divine inspiration. It was the
earliest heresy to trouble the Church, and brought out protests
from both St. Paul and St. John. It has been the constant
temptation of philosophic minds who want religion without as-
senting to dogma. So Spinoza, *Ep. xxi: Dico ad salutem non esse
omnino necesse, Christum secundum carnem noscere; sed de
aeterno illo filio Dei, hoc est, Dei aeterna sapientia quae sese in
omnibus rebus, et maxime in mente humana et omnium maxime
in Christo Jesu manifestavit, longe aliter sentiendum.* For the
rôle of docetism in the deist philosophy and its resuscitation
by Strauss, see A. S. Farrar, *History of Free Thought*, 191, 381,
613.

known and, with the exception possibly of Marcionism, the most important of the gnostic sects. The founder of this school, Valentine, the "Platonicus" as he is called by Tertullian, got his education in Alexandria, but was teaching at Rome in the middle years of the second century. Like other Gnostics, he began his theosophy with the problem *unde malum,*[22] and, again, like the others, resolved the difficulty by making an absolute divorce between the Infinite and the ill-conditioned finite, and then stopping up the breach with a series of intermediaries.

At the summit of Valentine's hierarchy stands the Bythos (Abyss) or Sigê (Silence). It is a question whether these are two entities or merely different names for the one inexpressible Absolute. I suspect that they represent the potentiality and actuality of the Aristotelian and the Stoic metaphysics. Thus Silence would be the potentiality (or *logos endiathetos*) within the Abyss of that which is to become actual in the intermediaries (as the *logos prophorikos*). At any rate from this Absolute by some process of devolution springs a series of Aeons in couples, named respectively: Nous

[22] Cf. Tertullian, *Contra Marc.,* i, 2; Eusebius, *Hist. Ec.,* V, xxvii; Epiphanius, *Pan.,* xxiv, 6.

(Reason) and Alêtheia (Truth), Logos
(Word) and Zôê (Life), Anthrôpos (Man,
i.e. the First or Divine Man) and Ekklêsia
(Church). These six Aeons, together with Bythos and Sigê according to some authorities, or
according to others with a fourth pair of emanations, form the Ogdoad. If we are to look
for any comprehensible meaning in this phan-
tasmagoria, probably Mansel is right in saying
that "the first order of Aeons, the Ogdoad, is
obviously intended to represent the Supreme
Being in two aspects: first, in his absolute nature, as inscrutable and unspeakable; secondly,
in his relative nature, as manifesting himself in
operation."[23]

From the Ogdoad springs a lower Decad of
five couples,[24] where, again quoting Mansel, the
masculine Aeons, with their feminine counter-
parts, "are clearly meant to represent that combination of unity with variety, of the infinite
with the finite, of identity with difference, which
is implied in the notion of derived and definite
existence." Third in order comes the Dodecad,

[23] Mansel, *The Gnostic Heresies*, 173. According to Tertullian,
Adv. Valentinianos, 36, some of the sectarians took these Aeons
simply as the attributes or names of God in His various activities as thinker, producer, etc.
[24] Bythios and Mixis, Agêratos and Henôsis, Autophyês and
Hêdonê, Akinêtos and Synkrasis, Monogenês and Makaria.

composed of six couples,[25] where the masculine terms designate God "in his religious relation towards man," while the feminine terms "represent the gifts of Grace which that relation conveys and implies." All of which may or may not be a true interpretation, but is certainly a generous attempt to discover sense where it scarcely seems to exist.

These three orders make up the divine Pleroma of thirty Aeons. And in that super-rarefied region of abstractions it should appear that something like the drama of our earthly life first takes place, and thus prepares the way for the passage from the invisible world to the world of material phenomena.

Unfortunately at this point our sources are sadly confused. But so much we can learn: that the whole miserable business of existence depends on the illicit desire of Sophia, the last of the thirty Aeons, to comprehend the being of the supreme Father, who can be comprehended, if by any, only by the highest emanation, the Nous. The tragic drama within the Pleroma would thus correspond to man's

[25] Paraklêtos and Pistis, Patrikos and Elpis, Mêtrikos and Agapê, Axinous and Synesis, Ekklêsiastikos and Makariotês, Thelêtos and Sophia. For other interpretations of these Aeons see F. Legge, *Forerunners and Rivals of Christianity*, II, 102.

trust in the lower wisdom of the senses to grasp
those transcendent truths which belong only to
the wisdom of divine insight. In the Pleroma
itself a recurrence of this fatal presumption is
forestalled by the emanation of a new power,
the Christ or the Holy Ghost, who restores the
Aeons to a state of equilibrium, while still
another Aeon called the Cross (or Horos, "limitation") is emitted to act as a boundary forever
enclosing and protecting the celestial sphere. In
their joy the Aeons now contribute each his
part to create a new Son, Jesus, who is the
spiritual expression of the whole Pleroma, the
result or the cause (the records are ambiguous)
of salvation to the heavenly Powers.

Meanwhile the unholy Desire of Sophia, having been ejected from the Pleroma, is endowed
by this Jesus with form, though without knowledge, and is personified as Achamoth (Aramaic
for Sophia, Wisdom). From the passion of her
nostalgia in the outer region of shadowy emptiness are born the elements of the phenomenal
world:—from her longing to return to God, the
soul of the world and the Demiurge; from her
laughter all that is bright; from her grief and
consternation the solid substance. Out of these,
in some way not clear to us, the Demiurge

(identified with the Jehovah of Scripture) fashions the lower order of existence with its host of evil daemons, and creates man, a psychic and material creature, in whose progeny abides a portion of the divine spirit which has descended to them from the Pleroma through Sophia and Achamoth.

The office of salvation is then to rescue this spark of the heavenly spirit from its entanglement in the psychic and material nature of humanity; and to this end the Christ, or the Jesus, of the Pleroma (or some other emanation of the same name) comes down to earth and dwells for a season amongst men as Jesus of Nazareth. But his body is a mere phantom and his semblance of mortal life a pure illusion. To those men who partake of the celestial nature, the *pneumatikoi*, he imparts the same sort of knowledge, or *gnôsis,* as that which restored the shaken Pleroma to equilibrium, so that at their death their spirits may escape to the heavenly home. The drama of redemption on earth is a repetition, so to speak, of what had occurred on high; but of any true incarnation, or of any salvation from sin by conversion of the repentant soul, there is nothing.

As pure poetry the system of Valentine

might elicit our admiration; there is in fact
something grandiose in this play of an irresponsible imagination with the fading myths
of the old world. It has, too, this value, that it
shows how desperately the mind of the Hellenistic peoples was wrestling with the problem
of evil and the need of salvation; and one clear
contribution, we must allow, it made to Christian theology,—the sense that the Incarnation
of the Logos was not an isolated event in the
history of the human race, but was rather a
single act of a cosmic drama wherein the spheres
of eternity and the very integrity of God are
mysteriously involved. So much we may grant.
But to take this jumble of superstitions grafted
on an impossible rationalism literally as a serious advance in religion, to discern in it a high
philosophy, and to laud the Gnostics generally
as more cultured and intelligent than the orthodox believers, seems to me to border on
pedantic madness. In contrast with the apologetic tone adopted by most scholars of the present day towards Gnosticism, influenced as they
often are by an unavowed desire to elevate each
and any rival of the Church, it is refreshing to
hear the words of old Burtogge, an obscure
philosopher of the seventeenth century:

"Those Discourses in which nor Words nor Propositions are sensible, or wherein the Words are sensible but not the Propositions, and yet are taken by those that make them for high Sence, may be called *Enthusiasm*. Of the former sort I apprehend the Whims of *Basilides,* of *Valentinus* and the *Gnosticks*; and of the latter, those of the *Familists,* and of others of late."[26]

Before leaving this subject a word should perhaps be said of a heresy which is commonly regarded as gnostic, but which, by its avoidance of intermediaries, its emphasis on ethics rather than on metaphysics, and its dependence on the Bible alone for its doctrine, stands apart from the Valentinian and other similar sects. Its founder, a certain Marcion of Pontus, came to Rome about the year 140, and for a while attached himself to the orthodox Church. But under the influence of a Syrian named Cerdo he developed a creed which soon brought him into conflict with the ecclesiastical authorities.

26 *Organum Vetus et Novum,* ed. by Margaret W. Landes, p. 16. As an illustration of the apologetic attitude prevalent today I may quote these words from C. E. Raven's *Apollinarianism,* p. 7: "In other respects, too, he (Irenaeus) was a learned man, though inferior in intellectual power and speculative ability to the great Gnostics whom he attacked." The state of mind that sets the vapourings of Valentine's theosophy above the "recapitulation theory" of Irenaeus is to me utterly incomprehensible.

This influence can be seen primarily in the
character of the ethical dualism taught by Marcion. Creation was not the work of the good
God, who dwells aloft in remote isolation, nor
of Satan, who is the lord of evil, but of the
Demiurge, the Jehovah of the Old Testament,
who is not essentially evil, nor yet essentially
good, but is qualified by a kind of illusory virtue
called justice. Under the old dispensation men
knew no other God than this just and judging
Jehovah, whose law was based on the principle
of retaliation, "an eye for an eye," and whose
rule of meting out penalities for disobedience
kept man revolving in a vicious circle of hatred
and evil. Then in the fulness of time from the
unknown God came the Son, whose mission it
was to reveal the true Father as the Lord, not
of justice, but of pure love and compassion.
Redemption therefore is not so much a conversion of the penitent soul from wrong-doing to
righteousness (*i.e.* justice) as it is a calling of
the soul from the service of Jehovah to trust in
the mercy of the hitherto unknown God; while
morality consists on the one hand in the absten-
tion from all acts that involve the soul more
deeply in the world of creation (for which reason marriage especially should be eschewed),

and on the other hand in the practice of a charity that condemns nothing and nobody.

The originality of the heresy lies in the fact that it was the earliest effort to eliminate from the teaching of Jesus all its sterner and more virile elements and to reduce Christianity to a religion of irresponsible sympathy. From the Gospels the Marcionites isolated such sayings as "love your enemies" and "present the other cheek," and made them the sole canon of ethics and the key to the understanding of the divine Being. Their creed might almost be summed up in the maxim that "God being good never punishes." The reply of the Church was on the one side to prove that the principle of love is not absent from the Old Testament, and on the other side to show that the teaching of Jesus by no means shirked the sterner law of retribution.[27] Marcionism thus represents a besetting temptation to reduce Christianity to a kind of effeminate humanitarianism; and it is highly significant that in these latter days one of the most prominent of the historians of dogma has openly avowed himself a disciple of this ancient semi-gnostical sect.[28]

[27] *Adamantius* (ed. Bakhuyzen), 118, 34, 28, 32.
[28] Adolph von Harnack, in the *Vossische Zeitung,* February 9 to 13, 1921.

CHAPTER III

THE CHRISTIAN THEOSOPHISTS

GNOSTICISM, whatever its faults and foibles, represents the effort of a troubled world to re-vivify the myths of a hoary antiquity with the breath of a living philosophy. To many at the time these convulsions of thought appeared to be, as they appear to some of today, the birth-pangs of a new religion; they were in fact the agony of death. To speak of Christianity as a favoured child of this movement is to misunder-stand the situation, as it seems to me, lament-ably; and the real problem of scholarship is not to explain how the disciples of Jesus, by selec-tion and rejection, put together so pure a cult from elements so distracted and grotesque, but rather to comprehend how such a cult, holding fast to the simple tradition of its origin, cut a way through the mythopoeic hurly-burly of the age and came out so little deflected from its course. A fair comparison of Christianity with

its boastful rivals offers the strongest of all
arguments for its unique claims, and, generally
speaking, the comparative study of religions,
often dreaded as a foe to the faith, tends really
to confirm the notion of a special revelation.

The distinction of the Church then would be,
not that it made a wiser adaptation than did its
adversaries of the three currents shaping the
thought of the age—this riot of metaphysics,
intermediaries, and superstition—but that it so
miraculously avoided them. We must, however,
while defending this assertion as true of the
essential nature of Christianity, make grave
reservations in regard to the attitude of certain
Doctors of the Church towards the insidious
temptation of metaphysics. What happened to
Philo in his endeavour to give a philosophical
basis to Judaism, happened also in some measure to the Fathers, notably to Clement and
Origen of Alexandria, whose appointed task it
was to create a sound *gnôsis* for the faith against
the false *gnôsis* of those who had usurped the
name. Thus to Clement, led on to meet his rivals
in their own high altitude, God becomes the infinite and unnamable One, rather the unthink-
able somewhat beyond the One and above unity
itself, even, in the dizzy language of Valentine,

the all-swallowing Abyss. God is not really the
Jehovah He is represented to be in the Law
and the prophets, capable of love and sympathy
and indignation, not really the Father as He
was known to Jesus, rejoicing over a repentant
sinner, nor the deity of John, compassionate to
the point of sacrificing His own Son for the salvation of mankind; but these feelings are only
attributed to Him by a kind of economy, in
condescension to human weakness, while in
fact He is eternally and absolutely *atreptos,*
without motion or emotion of any sort.[1]

It is clear that this conception of God has
been imported into religion from the monism of
the "heretical" philosophies; and that Clement,
profoundly Platonic as otherwise he was in
spirit, has suffered himself here to be carried
away by the tide which was leading on to the
transcendental inanities of Neoplatonism. And
it is equally clear that at bottom this conception
of God as seeming to have qualities which He
really has not is precisely an extension of the
docetic heresy which reduced the humanity of
Christ to mere appearance and the fact of his
Incarnation to a moral make-believe. Unfor-

[1] *Paid.,* I, viii, 7; *Strom.,* II, xvi. 73; V, x, 65; xi, 71; xii, 81,
et passim.

tunately, while the Church vigorously repudiated docetism in regard to the Son, it was se-
duced by the glamour of science falsely so called
into dealing leniently with the same error touching the Father. And still more unfortunately,
the rationalism of the Middle Ages sanctioned
the error as a dogma of the orthodox creed for
later times. As Baron von Hügel expresses it:
"Aristotle's conception of God's Unmoving
Energy is taken over by St. Thomas in the
form of God being One *Actus Purus*";[2] and
from that scholastic megalomania of the infinite
we have never recovered the lost ground of
common sense.[3] Excited by the mischief still
wrought by this fallacy of the reason William
James could exclaim: "The 'omniscient' and
'omnipresent' God of theology I regard as a
disease of the philosophy-shop."[4]

It may be said in excuse for these extravagances of theology that what the Fathers had
at heart was not the demonstration of a meta-

[2] *The Mystical Element of Religion*, II, 132.
[3] So the decree of the Vatican Council of 1870: "The Holy
Catholic Apostolic Roman Church believes and professes that
there is one living and true God, Creator and Lord of Heaven
and earth, omnipotent, eternal, immense, incomprehensible, infinite in intellect and will, and in all perfection; who being One,
singular, absolutely simple and unchangeable spiritual substance
is to be regarded as distinct really and in essence from the
world."
[4] *Letters*, II, 269.

physical theorem so much as a forcible expression of the surpassing majesty and sublimity of the divine person; that such terms as "infinite" and "omniscient" and "absolute" were rather the outpourings of the imagination before a stupendous mystery than the conclusions of a jejune dialectic, and were directed more to the practical end of worship than to the satisfaction of the imperious thinking power. On the side of reason also, as Gregory of Nyssa brings out so well,[5] our constant temptation in this plane of transient phenomena is to lose the stability of purpose and to float on the tides of chance, so that for our very salvation we need to raise our thoughts to something in the universe that is fixed and forever the same. For as our idea of God is, so do we tend to become. The otherworldliness and morality of religion both demand this intuition of unity within the many, of an immutable will behind the affections that change to meet a changing world, of character, let us say in a word, that alters not even "when it alteration finds."

No doubt it is possible on this ground to make allowance for the apparent inconsistency of a theologian like Augustine, when we find him

[5] *Or. Cat.*, 39.

on one page reasoning about God with the dry scholasticism suitable to a Plotinus and on another page attributing to the same God all that the most fervent, even anthropomorphic, worship could require. We may say, if we are charitably inclined, that his metaphysics is not the licence of reason but the superlative of reverence. And the same defence may be offered for St. Anselm, the Augustinian *par excellence,* who, while elaborating that nightmare of logic, the ontological proof of the being of God as that necessary something than which nothing can be conceived greater, will almost in the same breath write of a living Deity as different from the idol of the schools as a man's body is from its shadow cast on the wall.[6] So much we may grant to the imagination and the reason. Nevertheless it should not be forgotten that unity of character is something quite distinct from the abstract One of rationalism. The real God of Christianity is the object of veneration,—"the power not ourselves that makes for righteousness" if you like, but a power capable of responding to the appeals and confessions of the human heart, capable of feeling and purposing and thus in some measure subject

6 See the *Proslogion.*

to change, the enemy of evil and ugliness and lying and so in some measure limited, a personal Being whose will could be revealed through the incarnate Word. So far as the rationalized God of theology obscures this truth it is alien to the faith, a deplorable intrusion from the current of Hellenistic metaphysics. The problem of evil was forced upon the Church in an intolerable form by her lapse in this direction, and her humiliating contention with heresy sprang from the same source.

The failure to maintain a sharp boundary between monotheism and monism infected the higher theology at an early age, and is perhaps today the most serious obstacle in the way of a sound philosophy of religion. But, even so, it is still true that the error was of the nature of an excrescence which left the core of dogma intact; and this is proved by the fact that it did not lead to the creation of a divine hierarchy extending downwards from an absolute God through an intermediary half-god and so to the purely human. We touch here on a point of the utmost significance. There is no profounder mark of the originality of Christianity than its conception of the Logos as *becoming a mediator* between two natures instead of *existing as an interme-*

diary between two natures. We have seen how
Christ the Word is distinguished in this respect
from the gnostically coloured Word of Philo;
and we shall have occasion later to see how the
same distinction preserved the orthodox Christology from the most dangerous of all the heresies, Arianism.

No less significant is the fact that the usual
outgrowth of legends, which began at an early
date to cluster about the story of Jesus and retained a kind of subterranean life through the
Middle Ages, was peremptorily evicted from
the creed of the Church when the four Gospels
of our Testament were canonized and so set in
a different class from the Apocrypha. How close
and grave the peril had been, and how corre-
spondingly important the victory, only those
will appreciate who have studied the extant
fragments of the rejected literature. Thus, if
the so-called Gospel of Peter, which was read
in some churches as a work of apostolic authority, had been accepted, the dogma of an historical Incarnation might have been rarefied into a
shadowy docetism, and Christianity would have
been remembered merely as one of the innumerable gnostic superstitions. Elsewhere we have
incidents from the childhood of Jesus which are

not only rank with magic but artlessly immoral. For example the apocryphal Gospel of Thomas has these edifying tales:

"When Jesus saw what was done [a boy had broken down one of his water dams], he was annoyed and said to him, You mean and God-less ass, what harm did the pools and the waters do you? Now you shall wither like a tree. . . . And immediately the boy withered altogether."

"On another occasion Jesus was walking through the village, and a boy who was running knocked him on the shoulder. Jesus was furious and said to him, That is the end of your journey. And immediately he fell down and died."[7]

It is true the same high level of discrimination could not be kept everywhere amidst the corrupting influences of the world. Patristic literature, for instance, shows too plainly the gradual encroachment of an unwarranted reverence paid to Mary and the saints, ending in devotion to the Theotokos, or Mother of God, which gives to her, virtually if not admittedly, a place as intermediary in the divine Pleroma like that of the Great Mother in certain of the oriental sects.[8] The abuse of Mariolatry and

[7] A F. Findlay, *Byways in Early Christian Literature,* 174.
[8] In the fifth section of the *Sermo de Simeone et Anna,* attributed to Methodius, there is clear indication of the procedure by

hagiolatry became fixed in the liturgy and is
still defended by the Roman Church; it even
threatens to invade the extreme branch of
English catholicism. But we are here in the
region of exaggeration rather than of perversion; and no Christian will deny that a due
measure of homage may be rendered to the
mother of Jesus and to the great exemplars of
faith.

Perhaps the clearest cases of actual superstition admitted within the Church, or at least
tolerated by her, gather about the belief in
daemons, which in an innocent form goes back
to the Gospels but under the stress of the times
ran into extravagances as bizarre as they were
occasionally repulsive. The amusing side of this
daemonology may be seen in such stories as
that related of Gregory Thaumaturgus by his
more famous namesake of Nyssa.⁹ Now this
Gregory, a favourite pupil of Origen's, received
his surname from the wonders he wrought, and
one of these has to do with no less a personage
than Satan himself. The saint had been appointed bishop of Neocaesarea in Pontus

which the transcendental conception of God, including the
Logos, as τὸν τὰ πάντα ἐν ἀκαταληψίᾳ ὑπεριδρυμένον, has led to just
such an elevation of the Virgin Mary.
9 De Vita S. Greg. Thaum., 916 (Migne).

against his will, for he would have preferred a
life of solitary devotion, and was on his way to
take up his charge when the strange encounter
took place. Finding himself in a lonely country
at the fall of evening, he sought refuge in a
temple notorious thereabouts for its daemons
and its oracles. Here first he purged the edifice
of its evil occupants by the sign of the Cross, and
then passed the night, as was his wont, in praise
and prayer. At dawn he proceeded thence on
his way. But when the priest of the temple came
in the morning, he found the shrine deserted by
its familiars, and was told by them that no re-
spectable daemon could now enter; nor was he
able by all his lustrations and incantations to
drive out the aura of righteousness left behind
by the departed saint. Thereupon he set out in
pursuit of Gregory, and, on overtaking him,
poured out execrations and threats, because,
though a miscreant, he had dared to defile a
temple of the gods and by malignant arts had
destroyed the efficacy of the oracle. At last the
saint, to pacify and at the same time to humili-
ate the irate priest, consented to withdraw the
ban, and gave him a tablet with this inscription:
"Gregory to Satan, permission to enter." The
ticket proved more than valid; for the popula-

tion, learning that the daemons could inhabit their own sanctuary only at the good will of their enemy, argued that the Christian God was greater than Satan, and so were converted in a body.

Such stories are the natural byplay of the imagination and belong to the outlying fairy-land of faith; they are an almost inevitable expansion of that belief in the existence of spiritual power which is proper to Christianity as it is to all religion. But very early, it should seem, in the development of sacraments this daemonology laid special hold of the rite of baptism and turned it into an act of exorcism with consequences more serious to the Church. The candidate was obliged to enter the sacred piscina completely nude, divested of every article of clothing, jewel, amulet, or band for the hair which might harbour a daemon. Even with such precautions there was peril, and the enactment of the rite was attended by an ever increasing number of exorcists, so that at the Council of Arles in 314 most of the clerks who accompanied the bishops were functionaries of this sort. It was only with the spread of infant baptism that the sacrament gradually purified itself of these magical accretions, and an orthodox historian admits that the Roman liturgy still shows too evident traces of the ancient corruption.[10]

A critical reader may object that I have given a large place to superstition in a faith the characteristic note of which I have said to be just its purity in this respect. But if he will study the literature of the age, and compare the superficial vagaries of the Christian imagination with the monstrous absurdities imbedded in the very heart of Gnosticism, he will, I think, assent to my thesis. It is good to wring support from a foe, and so I would call the scoffing Lucian to witness. In his marvellous and apparently true story of a mountebank who filled the world with rumours of his miracles we read how the rogue, in connexion with his profitable traffic in oracles, established certain mysteries, and how at the beginning of the celebration a herald proclaimed these words: "If any atheist or Christian or Epicurean has come to spy upon our rites, let him depart!" Whereupon there was a general expulsion of these sceptics, while

[10] Duchesne, *Histoire de l'église,* III, 22. For an account of the method of baptism in the fourth century see Cyril of Jerusalem, *Catech.,* iii, 3, 4. It is a notable fact, as Bousset has shown (*Hauptprobleme der Gnosis,* 305), that few traces of the eucharist are found in Gnosticism, whereas its rite of baptism runs quite parallel with that of Christianity.

the celebrant cried, "Out with the Christians!"
and the multitude responded, "Out with the
Epicureans!"[11] It may seem strange to find the
followers of Christ and of Epicurus coupled
together in execration, but the union shows how
the Christians held aloof in sceptical contempt
from the current superstitions of the age. Individuals and separate communities no doubt
succumbed to the pressure of environment, but,
with the exception of Mariolatry and the kindred worship of saints, perhaps also of the
magic efficacy of baptism, the Church cut its
way cleanly through the surrounding murk or,
if it lost itself for a moment, soon recovered its
straight course. The notable truth, a truth of
incalculable significance, which forms in fact
the cardinal thesis for which I am contending,
is that in the Faith of Nicea and its expansion
at Chalcedon, *i.e.* in what may be called the
Constitution of Christianity as distinguished
from the creeds and the more fluctuating be-
liefs, the Church deliberately and emphatically
barred the intrusion of metaphysics into
religion with the attendant fallacy of intermediaries, and based the necessary dogma of faith
on a mythology free of superstition—unless

[11] *Alexander the False Prophet,* 38.

indeed the simple majestic fact of the Incarnation be so taken.

There was a long period of agony to be gone
through before that clearly defined position
could be reached. Meanwhile the first step was
to demonstrate against the cavilling of the edu-
cated that the faith of Christianity, its central
myth, was not unreasonable but conformed to
the deepest insight of the Greek tradition, was
in fact the final revelation of that for which
philosophy had been so long groping. To Paul,
in the first flush of battle and with his militant
temper, there should be no compromise: to the
believer God had made foolish the wisdom of
this world, while to the Greek the preaching of
Christ should be equally foolishness. The beginning of the reconciliation came with the fourth
Gospel, where the Greek terminology of the
logos is adroitly adapted to the Incarnation:
"The Word became flesh." From this memorable saying one group of the Apologists took
their cue, as we have seen in the passage from
Justin Martyr quoted above,[12] claiming for
themselves the true heirship of the Academy;
for, as the same writer declared, the dogmas of
Plato were not alien to Christ, and, as Athenag-

[12] See chap.. i, p. 9.

oras argued, the Ideas of Plato were a prophecy of the spiritual world, the heavenly inheritance, of the Christians.

But these were preliminary skirmishes; the real battle began when the Gnostics set about to construct a new religion by merging together a host of floating myths, with Christianity included on merely equal terms, and by suspending this grandiose scheme, so to speak, upon the Infinite Abstraction which was haunting the rationalistic minds of the age. Against this worldwide movement it was necessary to show (1) that Christianity was not one myth among many, but a divine revelation opposed to a swarm of superstitions, and (2) that its philosophy was the true *gnôsis* whose name had been falsely usurped by the enemy. In the first of these tasks St. Irenaeus, the Greek bishop of Lyons, took the lead; the second fell to Clement and to his successor in the school of Alexandria, Origen. The three writers, though of marked individuality, stand together in their aim, and form a group which may be designated as the Christian Gnostics, or theosophists.

The principal work of Irenaeus, the five books *Adversus Haereses,* published about the year 180 and for the most part extant only in a

Latin translation, falls into two sections, one
negative, exposing the madness of the gnostic
mystifications, particularly the Valentinian, the
other positive, setting forth the simple grandeur
of the Christian scheme of salvation. The latter
division of Irenaeus' work has thus an honourable place in literature as the earliest attempt at
a really constructive theology. Naturally it is
incomplete and inadequate, but it developed
and reiterated one capital idea which sank into
the Greek intellect and became the foundation
of all later reflection on the cause and purpose
of the Incarnation. The term which was to play
such a rôle in religious philosophy Irenaeus borrowed from St. Paul's Epistle to the Ephesians:
"Having made known unto us the mystery of
his will, according to his good pleasure which he
hath purposed in himself: that in the dispensation of the fullness of times he might *gather
together in one* all things in Christ." Here the
phrase underscored is a rather cumbrous translation of the single word *anakephalaiôsasthai,*
"to recapitulate," which to the critical reader of
antiquity, as we see in the commentary of St.
Chrysostom,[13] had a double meaning: (1) to
bring together the heads of a subject, to sum-

13 *In Ep. ad Eph.,* 8D.

marize, condense, and (2) to give a new head to
a thing, to restore, make over again. With these
meanings in mind Irenaeus connected the term
with another text from St. Paul: "For since by
man came death, by man came also the resurrection of the dead. For as in Adam all die, even so
in Christ shall all be made alive."

By applying these two meanings to *anakephalaiôsis,* "recapitulation," Irenaeus interpreted
the Incarnation as summing up in a single moment the long economy of God's dealing with
the world, whereby He purposed to restore men
to the place they had before the Fall, and thus
as rectifying, so to speak, by a new act of God's
will the failure of creation to fulfil its original
design. The method of the restoration is stated
succinctly by Irenaeus as follows:

"In times long past, it was said indeed that
man was created after the image of God, but
the fact was not clearly shown, for as yet the
Word after whose image man had been created
was invisible. And for this reason also man
easily lost the similitude. But when the Word
of God became (was made) flesh, he confirmed
and rectified both these matters: on the one
hand he showed forth the image in truth, by becoming himself that which was his image, and
on the other hand he reëstablished the similitude

after a sure manner, by assimilating man to the
invisible Father through means of the visible
Word."[14]

This is the answer of a Greek to the question
Cur Deus Homo; and, though the language is
borrowed from St. Paul, it moves in a direction
quite different from that taken normally by the
Latin mind under the influence of the dominant
Pauline doctrine, as exemplified in Anselm's
classical treatment of the theme.

In the beginning, Irenaeus says, having in
mind the false dualism of the Gnostics who held
the act of creation to be in itself a fault—in the
beginning man was made in the likeness of God
and was designed to be immortal, a being at
once human and divine. But because God Himself was not clearly manifest, being hidden in
His own invisible majesty, therefore man's hold
on the divine was precarious, and he was easily
tempted to forget his higher part and to sink his
interest to the lower element of his compound
nature. This was the Fall,whereby the celestial
similitude was marred and obscured, though
not obliterated; and thenceforth the purpose of
the divine economy is to restore man to his

[14] V, xvi, 1 (Harvey). The section should be read at length and
compared with such passages as IV, xi, 4; lii, 1; xxxiv, 6.

pristine glory by a progressive revelation of
the Creator in the phenomena of nature and
through the voice of lawgiver and prophet. At
the last comes the full and perfect epiphany.
The Incarnation is thus the conclusion and
epitome of the long process of history; it is also
an act of restoration. Always the Logos by his
title of Son possessed, potentially at least, the
nature of humanity, so that his birth in the flesh
is in a way no accident, but rather the fulfilment in time of the eternal "mystery of God's
will." On the other side man at the beginning
was endowed with a nature akin to the divine,
so that, seeing in Christ, as it were in a mirror,
the glory of God, he could be brought again to
realize what he had lost and to raise himself
once more to his higher destiny. "To this end
the Logos became man and the Son of God became the Son of man, in order that man, taking
in (*chôrêsas*) the Logos and receiving adoption, might become the son of God." For "how
should man pass to God, if God had not come
into man." It is thus: "As those who see the
light are within the light and partake of its
clarity, so those who see God are within God,
partaking of his clarity; the clarity gives them
life." Yet withal the light reveals to us not God

utterly in His most intimate being; but the love of God; it is love which by the Word leads us to God, and through obedience to the Word we learn ever more and more, and draw closer to the "mystery of his will." For "the Word of God, Jesus Christ our Lord, impelled by the immense love he bore us, was made even that which we are, in order that he might make us that which he is"; or, in the radiant phrase which became the motto of all later Christology. "God became man that men might become God."

The drama of salvation is thus in Irenaeus compounded of a double action, celestial and earthly, hints of which he may have borrowed from the very fables he was attacking, but purged of fantastic bombast and made practical for salvation by reference to a definite historical event.[15]

Some time about the year 150 there was born, probably at Athens, a certain Clement, called the Alexandrian from the place of his labours

---

[15] It is not easy to determine how far the doctrine of recapitulation in later authors derives directly from Paul and how far through Irenaeus. In Methodius, *Conv. decem Virg.*, III, iv, v, vi, for example, the theory is pushed to such a point that Christ appears to be actually identified with the person of the first Adam. Gregory Nazianzen, *Or.* II, 24, 25, carries out a minute comparison of the Fall with the Incarnation. See also Cyril of Alexandria, *In Joan.*, II, 481, 618, 620, 720, 730 (Pusey).

and in distinction to the Roman bishop of the
same name. Of his education we know thus
much, that somehow he acquired so wide an acquaintance with pagan literature that his quotations are one of our main sources of information in regard to many authors whose works are
lost. He himself tells us that he travelled about
from one instructor to another seeking the
truth until at last he met with Pantaenus, the
head of the Catechetical School at Alexandria.
It does not appear whether or not Clement was
already a confessing Christian at the time, but
in any case he stayed with Pantaenus, and in
due course succeeded him as master of the
school. In 202-3, on the outbreak of persecution
under Septimius Severus, he fled from the city.
He died, we do not know where, before the year
215.

In a word the public task of Clement might
be described as an endeavour to prove that
Christianity was the legitimate heir of Platonism, and therefore the possessor of a true philosophy against the claims of those who had perverted the doctrine of the Academy morally
and intellectually. He was the chief factor in
the effort, the tentative beginnings of which we
saw in "John" and in a few of the Apologists,

to amalgamate the inheritance of Israelitic prophecy in the gospel with the more noetic elements of the Greek tradition. To some scholars of today, notably to Harnack, this whole tendency was a mistake, and the assimilation of Christianity to Hellenic modes of thought resulted in a corruption of the faith rather than in a sound development. They wish that the young religion had eschewed reason and philosophy altogether, and had remained a simple code of life, such as, they suppose, Christ had desired it to be. I cannot for myself accept so narrow a view. Christianity, I think, could not have conquered the world had it not first conquered philosophy. Religion is not a fraction of life, not merely morality touched with emotion, as Matthew Arnold defined it to be, but the whole of life and the concern of all our faculties; and it would be a poor thing if it did not take into itself and remould the reason and the higher imagination. Nor, as I read the story, was the actual assimilation a betrayal or surrender of what was given in the gospel, since the Platonism adapted to the service of the new religion was congenial to its fundamental mythology and ethics. No doubt in the first approach to this great undertaking there were false motions and misunderstandings. Clement himself did not clearly discriminate between the functions of philosophy and of a presumptuous metaphysic, did not always discern the difference between the dualism of Plato and the monism which had captured the later Greek schools; he cannot, as we have already seen, be exonerated from his share in introducing that false conception of the nature of God which has never been entirely expunged from theology. But withal Clement beheld a great light, and, despite his wanderings and confusions, his activity is in a way, after the teachings of the fourth Gospel, the most dramatic moment spiritually in the history of our religion. The proper task of modern criticism would be, not to repudiate Clement and his successors in the Greek tradition, but to correct them where they went astray and to complete what they left unfinished, and so to make of Christianity a home adequate for the ever-questing spirit of man.

Besides a longish sermon there are extant three works of Clement which, with some cross currents, offer a progressive study of the Christian life. The first of these, the *Protrepticus,* or *Exhortation,* contains an eloquent contrast of the old worship with the new, and a call to conversion. The nobler ideas of the Greek poets, especially the tragedians, are not overlooked, but in the main the treatise presents a terrible indictment of the futilities and degradations of idolatry. We see, the lover of "the fair things of Hellas" sees with distress, how heavily the ancient world was weighted down by its superstitions, and how philosophy, without the succour of a new mythology, was powerless to reform the mass. Plato was aware of this stubborn fact, and had employed the resources of his royal imagination to the end of supplying the deficiency; but one feels in Clement how belief in the concrete event of the Incarnation had given him an emotional and effective sense of the reality of God and of spiritual truth beyond the reach of the most exalted individual genius.

The second work, the *Pedagogue,* is addressed to the converted, and deals with the Logos as guide and teacher (the *paidagôgos*) in the conduct of life. The book, apart from its purpose of edification, is interesting historically for its detailed picture of the morals and manners of a pagan city in Clement's day. Naturally the vanities of that society and its lust of pleasure are painted in dark colours, but on

the whole with less indignation than that of
Juvenal and less malice than that of Lucian;
while on the other hand the contrasted ideal of
Christianity is surprisingly free of morbid ex-
cess. The world, for those who live in it without
sinful attachment, is properly a place of joy
and innocence; prosperity is not condemned,
but welcomed, so long as it can be used for
noble ends and with a readiness always to lose
and suffer if need be. Our duty is not to root
out natural instincts, but to set a measure upon
them and to observe the right law of oppor-
tunity. As for the goodly display of nature, it
is to be enjoyed like flowers that delight the
eye. Only, while taking pleasure in the vision
of all things fair, we must not neglect to glorify
their Maker; nor must we forget that the unreserved abandonment of ourselves to their spell
brings certain remorse in its train, since too
quickly we learn that the fashion of this world
is but an ephemeral symbol of that which abides
and satisfies.[16] The tone of Clement in these
passages is not unlike that of the Platonism
carried on by the finer Stoics, and often one is
reminded of the beautiful saying of Marcus

[16] *Paid.*, II, v, 46; viii, 70.

Aurelius: "To look upon the charm of youth with chaste eyes."[17]

The principal work of Clement, that which gives him preëminence as a theologian, or, better perhaps, theosophist, is the *Stromata,* or *Stromateis* (the Patchwork). Here, passing from the naïver follies of idolatry, he makes a frontal attack on the sophisticated paganism of the Gnostics, which he scores as a kind of bastard offspring of the Academy. Their error, as he shows, is to fall into one or the other of two ethical extremes, antinomian or ascetic. For the former he takes as his example the followers of Carpocrates and of his son Epiphanes, that precocious youth who at the age of seventeen or earlier published a notorious treatise *Concerning Justice.* Clement criticises their doctrine as a false interpretation of Plato. They make justice a matter of mere equality and lack of distinctions (as heaven, they say, embraces all things impartially and God is the same to all men), whereas Plato actually defined justice as the art of dealing with men according to their merit and to the distinctions of virtue. So also in Plato's *Republic* the com-

---

[17] *Com.,* iii, 2: Καὶ τὸ ἐν παισὶν ἐπαφρόδιτον τοῖς ἑαυτοῦ σώφροσιν ὀφθαλμοῖς ὁρᾶν.

munity of wives was strictly regulated and was
devised rather to control desire than to foster
the sort of indiscriminate licence which the Car-
pocratians upheld. Clement thus goes out of
his way to defend the pagan philosopher
against his depraved disciples, but withal he is
not unmindful of the claims of Christianity. In
one place he makes a subtle distinction (though,
I think, not altogether tenable) between the
Greek and the Christian conception of self-
control (*enkrateia*) : the aim of the Greek was
to restrain evil desire from passing into act,
whereas the Christian sought to inhibit the evil
desire itself.[18]

For the other ethical extreme Clement turns
to the school of Marcion, and shows how their
false asceticism also arises from a misunderstanding. Plato taught that the creative work
of God was good as far as the resisting medium
permitted, and that the duty of man is to flee
from evil and to diminish its sway by participating actively in the divine purpose. Marcion
on the contrary, though regarding himself as a
genuine Platonist, held not only that evil was
inherent in the original matter of creation, but
that the act of creation itself, that is to say the

[18] *Strom.*, III, ii, 5, 10; iii, 12, 19, 21; v, 40; vi, 45; vii, 57; V, i, 3.

attempt to impose order and law upon the chaotic mass, was the mistaken energy of a lower deity. Hence the duty of man, as his salvation, is to take no part in the prolongation of the world but to hasten its end by refraining from marriage and by withdrawing so far as possible from all physical life. Here again Clement takes part with Plato against the Gnostic in rejecting a false asceticism; but himself differs from Plato in regarding the world as created *ex nihilo,* and hence in attributing the origin of evil to the free will of man rather than to some necessity in the nature of things.

In general Clement's attitude towards philosophy is clear and consistent; it may be pretty well summed up in the sentence: "The Hellenic philosophy by cleansing and moralizing the soul prepares it for the reception of faith, on which the truth builds up knowledge (*tên gnôsin*)."[19] This progress, then, or upbuilding of the soul in faith is the larger theme of the *Stromata* and Clement's chief contribution to religious psychology. His formula is taken from Paul's "faith, hope, charity," except that in place of the last term he is wont to substitute its equivalent in his vocabulary, "knowledge."

19 *Ibid.,* VII, iii, 20.

Faith to Clement is primarily the intuition of God from the observation of nature. For, looking out on the glories spread over the face of the earth and poured down from the heavens, what eye can fail to see the signs of a divine artificer? In the world's Sabbath of beauty it is, in the exquisite phrase of our author, as if we actually beheld God "resting in joy upon the finished work of His hands."[20] Faith is the very reverse of atheistic pessimism: "Alas for the evil mind of the Gnostics, who blaspheme the will of God and the mystery of creation, slandering this visible world." On the other hand, faith is equally opposed to the spirit of idolatry which leads men to worship the creature instead of the Creator, and to the pantheism which merges creature and Creator into one indistinguishable mass. Faith is the golden mean found by those who admire the visible world but sanctify their wonder by recognition of the invisible Maker to whom it raises them. Clement agrees with the vigorous assertion of St. Paul in the first chapter of Romans, that faith is implanted in all men by grace; but he would differ from the Apostle in allowing to

[20] *Ibid.*, II, ii, 6: Ἐπαναπαύεται δὲ τερπόμενος τῇ δημιουργίᾳ.

philosophy a larger part in the discovery and evolution of truth.[21]

This initial stirring of faith is a gift of the Logos, the teacher who from the beginning has spoken to all races of men from the world and in the still small voice of conscience. It is a kind of involuntary assent to the suggestion of the eternal everywhere present behind the veil of these transient forms; but it is not possession of that presence, nor alone does it impart the full peace and joy that belong to possession. For this there is needed the element of hope introduced by the Incarnation, whereby we are enabled to believe that, as the Logos endured the restriction of human nature, so we may be raised to partake of the divine nature. Hope also, like faith, is a gift from above, but under its impulse man is not merely a passive recipient; hope is a summons to act, and for growth in grace the voluntary coöperation of all our faculties is required. Thus by hope faith is transformed into an aggressive principle of conduct; it lends power to control the temptations of the flesh, for the believer is now persuaded of things to come and still invisible that they are closer to him, more really present, than

21 *Ibid.*, III, xvii, 102; IV, xxiii, 148.

what lies at his feet.[22] By the same motive we
are led to bestir the mind from inert revery to
the energy of true contemplation and study.
Clement, like Plato, was no despiser of secular
wisdom as an aid to spiritual intuition, and he
would have the prospective Gnostic trained in
the science of the schools and in discernment of
his own heart. "We admit," he says, "that a
man can be a believer without learning, but we
also assert that without learning he cannot
really comprehend the things which are declared to him in the faith"; and again, "He that
knoweth himself shall know God."[23] So at the
last, through the stimulation of hope, faith is
transmuted into knowledge, and the simple believer grows into the mature Gnostic.

A considerable part of the *Stromata,* particularly the seventh book, is devoted to the por-
trayal of such a Christian, and no analysis of
these pages can convey an adequate notion of
the richness of Clement's ideas and the depth of
his religious experience. Yet if one asks what
specifically the true Gnostic knows and how his
knowledge differs from mere belief, the answer
is not easy. The change in fact is rather in

22 Cf. the πόθος τῶν μὴ παρόντων repudiated by Epictetus and the
Stoics. See also Greg. Nys., *De Hom. Op.,* xxii.
23 *Strom.,* I, vi, 35; *Paid.,* III, i, 1.

definiteness and assurance than in substance: the vague sense of the supernatural has become gradually a living reality with which our soul has immediate communion, and the intellectual conviction of philosophy has been converted into the possession of religion. Truth for Plato, Clement says, lay in the Ideas of justice and beauty and the like, whose being can be inferred from their operation in the world while they themselves dwell in remote isolation; but to the Christian these Platonic Ideas are known as the eternal Word of God which has been uttered in the process of creation, and at the last made manifest in the flesh. "I am the truth," said Christ, and in that sentence the hard problem that had so vexed Plato's philosophy seemed to be solved. We need no longer inquire how phenomena participate in Ideas, or look for the bond between the abstract and the concrete, the universal and the particular; in the person of Jesus the two are actually brought together dynamically by the union of his divine and human nature, and truth has been made, as it were, visible and imitable.[24]

Thus, though Clement regards the progress of the Christian as a growth in knowledge and

24 *Strom.*, V, iii, *et al.*

though at times his theology seems to be floating off into the transcendental abyss, he is far
from being an intellectualist in the arid sense
of the word, and he can speak with biting scorn
of the eristic of the schools. Perhaps his favourite text from all the Bible is the beatitude,
The pure in heart shall see God; and he never
forgets that reflection on the mysteries of philosophy is barren of fruit unless there goes with
it *pari passu* a cleansing of the windows of the
breast, whereby the soul may look out and the
light of heaven may look in. Bathed in that
celestial radiance, the life of the Gnostic is
described as a continuous state of prayer, not
in petitioning for this or that blessing, but in
what may be called an uninterrupted intercourse with God.[25] His days are an unbroken
festival; for he is persuaded that, whether he
barter in the market-place or journey by sea
or travel in strange lands, the Master of all is
everywhere about him, able to hear and ready
to respond. On such a man the allurements of
the flesh and its passions have lost their hold;
he has attained the true apathy, which is not the
callous indifference of the Stoic, but joy in the

25 Cf. Plato, *Laws*, 716D: Προσομιλεῖν ἀεὶ τοῖς θεοῖς εὐχαῖς. This becomes the regular formula for prayer; see *Religion of Plato*, 294.

unsated contemplation and unhindered service
of the ever-present Friend. And as the com-
pany of a good man, through the reverence he
inspires, draws us on to imitate his virtues, so
the Gnostic is lifted ever more and more into
the similitude of that which he adores, until it
is possible to say of him that in a manner he has
become God.[26]

In the end knowledge and love are thus con-
vertible terms, as indeed from the beginning
the seeker after knowledge was led on by that
which is lovable in the object of his faith.[27] The
true *gnôsis,* which the sectarians have thought to
evoke out of the metaphysics and superstitions
of a deluded world, is nothing more than the
consummation of St. Paul's trinity of faith,
hope, and charity.

The last and, in some respects, the greatest
of the Christian theosophists was Origen, great
as a man, as a philosopher, as a scholar, stupendous in his unremitting industry. He was
born of Christian parents at Alexandria in 185.
When only eighteen he succeeded Clement as
head of the Catechetical School, and from that
time, indeed from infancy almost, his life was

26 *Strom.,* VI, ix; VII, vii; IV, xxvi, 171; IV, xxiii, 149.
27 *Ibid.,* VII, ii, 10.

devoted, as few other lives have been, to the incessant toil of learning and teaching. His relations with the bishop of Alexandria were not always easy, and in 231 he finally quitted the city. Under Decius he suffered torture and imprisonment, and died in 254 at Tyre, where his tomb for many centuries was an object of veneration.

During his exile Origen taught for a time at Caesarea in Palestine, and from one of his pupils, Gregory the Wonder-Worker, we have a panegyrical oration which gives a vivid account of the method of instruction pursued. So eloquent was the master, so filled with awe for the knowledge he was imparting, that it seemed to the young scholar—he was but a boy when on his way to the law school at Berytus he met Origen—as if the word spoken was no other than the Holy Word of Christian worship. So ardent a love, he says, came upon him for the new wisdom, that he was induced to give up home and friends and the ambition of the courts; thenceforth he had but one passion—philosophy and the godlike teacher who had opened to him this revelation of the truth. Theology, the knowledge of God, was the final purpose of the lecturer, but to that end all

human learning was made to contribute.
"Therefore," Gregory adds, "there was no subject forbidden to us; nothing hidden or inacces-
sible. We were allowed to become acquainted
with every doctrine, barbarian or Greek, on
things spiritual or civil, divine or human, traversing with all freedom, and investigating the
whole circuit of knowledge, and satisfying ourselves with the full enjoyment of all the pleasures of the soul."[28]

The programme is large and inspiring. But
with all his erudition Origen was in a sense a
man *unius libri*. His attempt to produce an ac-
curate text of the Bible by publishing the current Greek translations of the Old Testament
in parallel columns with the Hebrew was, considering the means at his disposal, a task of
prodigious difficulty; it cost him years of labour, and the loss of this work, except for
pitiable fragments, is perhaps the heaviest ca-
lamity in the history of biblical scholarship. Of
his interpretation of the text, carried out in
innumerable commentaries and sermons, one is
obliged to speak with more reserve. Here he
undoubtedly believed that he was walking in

---

[28] *Or. Pan.*, 15, quoted by Westcott in his *Essays in the History
of Religious Thought in the West*. The closing words are memorable: Καὶ ἀπολαύουσι τῶν τῆς ψυχῆς ἀγαθῶν.

the footsteps of St. Paul,[29] and his belief was justified in so far as the Apostle himself had adopted the tortuous methods of his rabbinical masters. But in fact Origen's exegesis of Scripture is an exact counterpart of Philo's endeavour to find in Moses the fountain of his Jewish Platonism.[30] In both cases the Bible, in the language of Origen, was turned into "a vast sea of mysteries,"[31] over whose perilous depths the only guide was the glimmering star of allegory: "for the letter killeth, but the spirit giveth life." By this riot of allegory, employed without discrimination, almost, one might say, without conscience, the plain facts of history simply vanish out of sight and leave behind only a thin web of symbols and signs which the reader may understand very much as he chooses. So far did Origen go in this direction as to hold that certain passages of questionable morality or apparent inveracity were deliberately inserted in obedience to the Holy Ghost in order, as it

29 See, *e.g. In Genes. Hom.*, vii, 2; x, 5.
30 According to Photius (*Bibl.*, 105) the whole allegorical method of interpretation was borrowed by the Christians from Philo. The mischievous character of the procedure was not overlooked by critics from the Antiochene side, and Porphyry did not forget it when scoring the Christian school of philosophy. See also the tractate *De Placitis Manichaeorum*, Migne, P. G. XVIII, 417.
31 *In Genes. Hom.*, ix, 1: *Qui exigui meritis et ingenio tenues inire tam vastum mysteriorum pelagus audemus.*

were, to pry the mind away from the letter and force upon it the need of searching for concealed meanings. Naturally the results of such a system were often fantastic, as when, for example, the polygamy of the patriarchs is smoothed out into an allegory of the possession of the various virtues and Solomon's harem becomes a lesson in modesty. It is all very extravagant, sometimes funny, sometimes rather dubious ethically.[32]

It is not within the plan of this book to give a full account of the religious philosophy which Origen constructed upon the basis of such an exegesis, a subject, indeed, still needing more careful elucidation than it has received from historians of the period.[33] In a word it may be said, I think, that both the strength and the weakness of his views are conditioned by his immersion in the stream of speculation which was making for Neoplatonism; and Neoplatonism, despite its avowed hostility to the contemporary gnostic schools, was at heart only a refined and rationalized scion of the same

[32] So, *e.g.* in the twentieth sermon on Jeremiah he is forced to play fast and loose with the virtue of truthfulness.
[33] The lack may possibly be supplied when we get the second volume of De Faye's *Origène*. Meanwhile the best we have is Redepenning's somewhat antiquated work.

brood. At an early age Origen was a hearer of
that shadowy figure, Ammonius Saccas, from
whom Plotinus also got the germ of his metaphysical system. How far Origen was directly
influenced by his pagan teacher, we have no
means of knowing; we can only say that in the
main his philosophy may be described as an
honest and partly successful endeavour to
adapt the theosophy of the time to the fact of
the Incarnation and to the traditional dogmas
of the Church.

To Origen the Father was an infinite abstraction, scarcely distinguishable in theory
from the Absolute One of Plotinus, though
something of the warmer emotion of worship
tells us that we are still in the sphere of religion
and have not soared into the vacuity of pure
speculation. Of the Logos he writes often very
much in the vein of Philo, as if it were the semi-
hypostatized power of God going forth in the
act of creation, or were a kind of intermediary
through which the Infinite comes into contact
with the finite, and by which the human intelligence is raised into harmony with the divine.
Elsewhere the Logos is virtually identical with
the Nous of Plotinus, being the first emanation
from the overflowing One. But it is to Origen

also that Christology owes the accepted definition of the Word as "the eternally begotten
Son," and as "consubstantial" with the Father.
Hence it happened that, in the debates of the
fourth century, Athanasius and the great Cappadocians could go to Origen for phrases expressing a subordination of the Son to the
Father quite within the limits of orthodoxy,
while the Arians and other sectaries could appeal to his works for justification of their views
of the Logos as a mere intermediary.

Besides the Logos there was in Origen's
scheme a host of spirits, not begotten like the
Son but created. Their proper joy and function
was to dwell in the vision of their Maker; but
such contemplation of what is higher in nature
requires a constant and active exercise of the
will; and here, in the consequent defection of
the creature from the divine purpose of creation, Origen introduced a conception which was
to be developed by Athanasius into the profoundest of the orthodox theories of evil. By a
quaint pun on the words *psychos,* "cold," and
psyche, "soul," Origen explained the descent
from the spiritual to the lower psychical state
as a kind of refrigeration of zeal, correspond-

ing to the second emanation of Plotinus.[34]
Beside the Logos and the spirits who remained faithful to their high calling, there is
now a race of fallen and sinful souls, for whom
this material world is fashioned as a place of
retribution and discipline—hence the disasters
and apparent injustices of our mortal life. We
are here to suffer and to learn; yet not abandoned, though we have forfeited our birthright.
Among the souls of men one only keeps its
perfect purity and unworldliness, and upon this
elect soul the Logos, as the Holy Ghost, de-
scends, and so unites it to himself that Jesus
becomes Christ the Saviour. By his example
men are brought back to knowledge of their
original condition of grace. In the fulness of
time, Origen hints, there shall be a complete
"restoration," not only of these embodied souls
but of Satan and the other rebel spirits who, for
what reason we do not know, have not been
incorporated. Then God shall be all in all.

It is a lofty philosophy which Origen has
wrested from the enemy. But unluckily for his
fame, though he rejected the more puerile superstitions of a Valentine and the anti-Hebraic

[34] This fanciful etymology was not invented by Origen. See
Aristotle, *De Anima*, I, ii, 23, and Scott's *Hermetica*, I, 464.

theology of a Marcion, yet in his opposition to
these Gnostics he did not entirely escape the
contamination of their influence, nor was his
doctrine otherwise altogether free of dubious
elements.[35] Always he proclaimed himself an
obedient servant of the tradition; but in fact
his fault was to strike out too boldly into un-
tried ways of thought and to systematize the
faith before the time for system had arrived.
Hence to the Church he was, almost from the
beginning, an object at once of admiration and
of fear. Jerome, who owed much to his works,
first lauded him as "the master of the churches
after the Apostles," and then later, when his
own orthodoxy as a follower of Origen was im-
pugned, abused him as a corrupter of the faith.
And in the sixth century, the Emperor Justinian, "the Diocletian of theological science and
the Constantine of scholasticism," as Harnack
calls him, the zealot who closed the philosophical schools at Athens, the foe of error who yet
played fast and loose with the fundamental
dogma of Chalcedon, procured the final condemnation of Origen as a heretic. In the Middle
Ages it was a moot question whether the mighty

[35] To Origen the enemies of the Church were still Basilides and
Valentinus and Marcion. See, *e.g. In Jerem. Hom.*, x, 5; xvii, 2.

Alexandrian, along with such others as Samson, Solomon, and Trajan, was saved or eternally damned. Our consciences are not so tender, and we can afford to admire without fear of the rumblings of an uneasy orthodoxy. But withal a candid student today must admit that, if Origenism had prevailed without check, Christianity would have become rather a noble branch of theosophy than a living religion. Between the two great doctors Clement, though in many respects a lesser figure than his successor in the Alexandrian school, stands on the whole for a sounder blend of Platonism and Christianity, and is still for us the richer mine of spiritual philosophy.

CHAPTER IV

THE SETTING OF HERESY

THE three great contentions of the early
Church, as has been said, were with the pagan
world, with Gnosticism, and then with heresies
within herself. It was the task of the Apologists
to justify Christianity against the attacks of
paganism; and the champions of the second
conflict were the group of writers whom I have
called the theosophists, and of whom Irenaeus,
Clement, and Origen were the successive leaders. Victory in these two fields came not at once,
but with prolonged and renewed struggles. The
most searching persecutions fell after the voice
of the Apologists was silent and just before the
final surrender of the world; and so Maniche-
ism, essentially a late gnostical sect, was powerful enough in the fourth century to enthral the
youthful Augustine for nine years and through
him to leave its stamp on the western Church.
The service of Mithra also, which by its hold on

the army might be called a revival of paganism
and at the same time had many gnostical features, spread widely in the third and fourth
centuries, though, curiously enough, it is seldom
mentioned by the Christian controversialists.[1]
Nevertheless all this while the Church was the
growing power, the bearer of the seed of the
new civilization, and with the conversion of
Constantine it became definitely the master; its
old enemies were silenced or put on the defensive. Then arose the enemy within. From the
very beginning there had been divisions; so that
we find St. Paul in the earliest of his epistles
anathematizing those who "would pervert the
gospel of Christ," and St. John in his letters
protesting against the docetic dissolution of the
faith into a kind of make-believe. But there is no
binding force like that of a common fear and a
common foe; and while the secular world and
Gnosticism were arrayed against the Church,
the enemy within the gate could make little
headway. The change came in the fourth century; the years from the Council of Nicea to the

---

[1] Since Cumont's great work on the subject it has been the
fashion to make a great deal of Mithraism as a rival of Christianity, and no doubt the worship was widespread. But, taking
account of the infrequent mention of the subject in the literature of the age, I am inclined to think that the danger from this
source has been exaggerated.

Council of Chalcedon are marked by a civil war
with heresy which threatened the very existence of Christianity as an organized religion.

Heresy was like the fabled Hydra, which,
when one head was cut off, threw out two in its
place, or like Proteus, who when grasped in one
form melted away into another. The unwarned
reader of the history of that period, lost in the
maze of definitions and counter definitions,
may well cry out that the whole affair was no
more than a senseless logomachy. But in fact
through all their ramifications the heresies of
the age—at least those that really counted—
revolved about a single article of the faith and
can be arranged in a simple pattern. The
reader will have an effective clue to the labyrinth if he will hold fast to the following four
principles:

There was no dogma of a trinity of persons
in the primitive Church, and this dogma was
never, in our period, anything but an intellectual overgrowth of secondary importance.

But from the beginning the Church held the
belief in Christ as a person in some way both
human and divine.

The real problem of theology was thus not
the Trinity, but the reconciliation of a second

divine personality with the monotheism of the Old Testament.

And, finally, this problem was distorted and rendered unnecessarily acute by the merging of Hebrew monotheism with a rationalistic monism.

There can be no proper understanding of the movement we are about to study until the vexed question of the Trinity is laid, and that salutary ground cannot be reached until the date and cause of the personification of the Holy Ghost are settled—at least for us. Now, to begin with, I think an unprejudiced student of the New Testament must arrive at this conclusion, that (1) to Jesus himself the Holy Ghost was not a person distinct from the person of the Father, and that (2) the Bible as it stands gave to the infant Church no trinitarian *dogma,* though it did contain a trinitarian *formula.*

(1) The most indubitable utterance of Christ in regard to the Holy Ghost is that in Mark iii, 28-30, where, replying to the Scribes who had accused him of casting out devils by the prince of the devils, he declares:

"Verily I say unto you, All sins shall be forgiven unto the sons of men, and blasphemies wherewith soever they shall blaspheme:

"But he that shall blaspheme against the

Holy Ghost hath never forgiveness, but is in danger of eternal damnation:

"Because they said, He hath an unclean spirit."

Certainly the Holy Ghost here is no more than the *ruach* of the Old Testament, the indwelling spirit of God by which His will was known to the prophets, and through which, as elsewhere in the Gospels, Jesus claims to be in special communion with the Father. To blaspheme the spirit is the unpardonable sin because such an act is to reject the voice of God speaking in the heart and to cut one's self off from all contact with the divine influence. To make of the Holy Ghost a separate person and so to imply that one may be pardoned for blaspheming the person of the Father, but cannot be pardoned if he blasphemes the person of the Holy Ghost, is to reduce the words of Christ to something worse than nonsense. The expansion of the saying in Matthew xii, 32 and Luke xii, 10 avoids indeed that gross error, but rather weakens the claim of Christ to a peculiar union of his own spirit with the spirit of God.

(2) Nor is the Holy Ghost anywhere else in the New Testament so personified as to warrant the trinitarian dogma found in the so-

called Nicene Creed.[2] Twice, however, we do
find a trinitarian formula, that is to say, we find
the Holy Ghost added to the names of the
Father and the Son as an aspect of their power
so unique as to be designated by a separate
title. The earliest passage in which such a
formula occurs is the second Epistle to the
Corinthians, which closes with the benediction
of St. Paul, as follows: "The grace of the Lord
Jesus Christ, and the love of God, and the communion of the Holy Ghost, be with you all."
Now in the first place, whatever may be said of
Paul's conception of the divine personality of
Christ, it is clear from other statements in
his epistles that he did not think of the Holy
Ghost as a separate person. For instance, in
1 Cor. ii, 10-16, the spirit that searcheth all
things and makes known to us the things of God
so that we are raised to spiritual sonship, cannot
be personified, unless by the same token "the
spirit of man" is also hypostatized as a person
apart from the man himself. What Paul had
in mind may be understood from the similar
benediction in Revelations i, 4, 5: "Grace be
unto you, and peace, from him which is, and
which was, and which is to come; and from the

2 For the evidence see Appendix B.

seven Spirits which are before his throne; and
from Jesus Christ, who is the faithful witness."
The seven spirits manifestly are a poetical figure for the power of God poured out upon
the seven churches, the *ruach* communicating
between heaven and earth. And so in Paul the
"communion" of the Holy Ghost, or the "fellowship" as it is rendered in the Prayer Book,
is but another way of expressing the outflowing
love and grace of the Father and the Son.

Now drop from Paul's benediction the words
"grace" and "love" and "communion," and you
have the baptismal formula put into the mouth
of Jesus at the end of Matthew. There are grave
doubts of the authenticity of this verse,[3] and for
my part I cannot believe that it gives the actual
words of Jesus. They seem too manifestly a
late expansion of the original form of the rite as
it is described in Acts xix, 5, 6: "They were
baptized in the name of the Lord Jesus; and
when Paul had laid his hands upon them, the

[3] The current form of the command as given in Eusebius is
simply: "Go ye and teach (make disciples of) all the nations in
my name," and some critics hold that to be the original form,
of which the Matthean text is an amplification. This view is
supported by Peter's and Paul's formula of baptism in (or into)
the name of Christ only (Gal. iii, 27; Rom. vi, 3; 1 Cor. i, 13, 15;
Acts ii, 38; viii, 16; x, 48); and it is hard to accept the text of
Matthew as rendering the actual words of Jesus. But that is not
the question here. Whatever its source, the trinitarian formula
was read at least by most Christians in their Gospel.

Holy Ghost came on them." But however this may be, the passage, though it is still not dogma in the sense that it necessarily personifies the Holy Ghost, undoubtedly looks in that direction, and is the point of transition from Paul's trinitarian formula of benediction to the theological Trinity of the Nicene Creed.

The steps by which this transition occurred can be made out pretty clearly in the writings of the Apologists. In their first fumbling attempts to create a theology these writers all built on one firm belief, that the Christ, through whom came the knowledge of God, was in some way himself divine, that the validity of the revelation depended on the revealer's peculiar kinship with God. In the New Testament they found two terms specially used to define such kinship, the "Son," which was the expression chosen by Jesus himself, and the "Logos," which was introduced by the author of the prologue to the fourth Gospel. This latter term was undoubtedly suggested by its usage in Greek philosophy, but it could be justified also, as we have seen, by Biblical texts, particularly by the formula of creation in Genesis, "And God said," where the act of saying might be personified, so to speak, as the uttered Word going

forth from God with creative energy. Now
Logos of itself, or even combined with the term
Son, would have possessed for the Christians,
as for Philo, only a kind of metaphorical personification, were it not for the additional phrase,
"The Word became flesh." That made a world
of difference. By identification with the historical Jesus the Logos became immediately the
Son of God as a living concrete person. The
theology of the Apologists therefore begins
with the startling dogma of two persons in the
deity, Father and Son, God and His uttered
Word,—startling certainly to any disciple of
the Old Testament, but again justified by reference to the phrase of creation, "Let *us* make,"
which was interpreted literally as conversation
between two persons.

But besides the Word, which had thus been
definitely personified by application to the Son,
there were other similar expressions in the Old
Testament, such as "spirit" and "wisdom,"
which had undergone no such sea change and
might remain as vague names for the power of
God exercised on and in the world. Hence in
the Apologists we find this rather puzzling, but
really quite natural, phenomenon. Frequently
(1) Word and Spirit and Wisdom are regarded

as synonymous and are identified singly or in combination with the Son, in such a manner that we have a clear dyad of persons with no suspicion of a Trinity. At other times (2) the personification of the Word in the New Testament, taken with the unpersonified use of Spirit and Wisdom in the Old Testament, leads to a kind of trinitarian formula, in which the Spirit or Wisdom is joined to the two persons as a poetical, or semi-hypostatized, symbol of their effluent power, just as in the Old Testament they were so attached to the Father alone.[4] This is quite in the tone of Paul's trinitarian formula of benediction. And then, at other times, (3) the formula has the ring of dogma and, if read by itself, would suggest that the writer had in mind a distinct trinity of persons. Perhaps even more commonly we find the three stages in the growth of dogma confused together. A few quotations will show how these three views could exist side by side in the same mind.

Justin Martyr:—

(1) "Moses the aforesaid prophet has taught

[4] This ambiguity is the ultimate source of the division between the eastern and western Churches over the question whether the Spirit proceeds from the Father alone or from both the Father and the Son (*filioque*).

us that by the Spirit and the Power from God we must understand nothing but the Word, who also is the first-born of God; and this Spirit coming upon the virgin and overshadowing her, not by ordinary intercourse but by power, caused her to conceive." (*Apol.* I, xxxiii.)

(2) "We worship and adore both Him and the Son who come from Him and taught us this doctrine; also the host of good angels who follow and resemble him, and the prophetic Spirit." (*Ibid.,* I, vi.)

(3) "We worship the Creator of the world. . . . As for Jesus Christ, who was our teacher of this doctrine and to this end was born and crucified, . . . we know that he is truly the Son of God and we hold him in the second place. The prophetic Spirit we honour in the third rank." (*Ibid.,* I, xiii.)

Athenagoras:—

(1 and 2) "We acknowledge a God, and a Son His Word, and a Holy Spirit, united in power,—the Father, the Son, the Spirit, because the Son is the mind and word and wisdom of the Father, and the Spirit is an effluence as light from fire."[5] (*Supp.,* 24.)

(3) "Who then would not be astonished who hear those men called atheists who affirm God

---

[5] Elsewhere, § 10, this spiritual effluence, which spoke through the prophets, is described as flowing from God and returning back to Him like a beam of the sun.

the Father and God the Son and a Holy Spirit, and who demonstrate their power in unity and their distinction in rank." (*Ibid.,* 10.)

Theophilus:—

(1) "God begot him along with His wisdom before all things. He had this Word as a helper in His Work. . . . He then, being Spirit of God, and governing principle, and wisdom and power of the Highest. . . ." (*Ad Autol.,* ii, 10.)

(2) "God by His own word and wisdom made all things; for 'by His word were the heavens made, and all the host of them by the breath of His mouth.' Most excellent is His wisdom. . . . To no one else but to His own Word and Wisdom did He say, 'Let us make'." (*Ibid.,* i, 7; ii, 18.)

(3) "The three days which preceded the creation of the luminaries are a type of the Trinity —of God, and His Word, and His Wisdom." (*Ibid.,* ii, 15.)

A fair reading of the Fathers of the second century shows, I think, that, through all the fluctuations of their language, what they really had in view can be expressed by a trinitarian formula in which the Holy Ghost is not personified (as in the later trinitarian dogma), but added to the Father and the Son as a name for their effluent power and sympathy.

Hippolytus has in fact stated the position of the age in the clearest and most unmistakable language:

"I will not say two Gods, but one God and two persons, and a third economy which is the grace of the Holy Ghost (*i.e.* and there is a third thing, the grace of these two going out in the government of the world as their holy spirit). For the Father is one, but there are two persons, since the Son also is one, and the third is the Holy Ghost." (*Contra Haer.*, xiv.)

And this is precisely the thought of the Apostles' Creed, where belief in the Son is carried out into the full language of personality, while the Holy Ghost is relegated to the same class of impersonal objects of belief as the Church, the Communion of Saints, etc. It was manifestly the doctrine of Paul. But a triad of deities was a common feature of that mythopoeic age, and this influence made itself gradually felt in Christianity. Theophilus was the first of the Fathers to employ the actual word "trinity" (*trias*), but it remained for a Latin brain to petrify the fluid thought of the Greeks into a sharply defined, legally expressed dogma. To Tertullian we owe the attribution of the term "person" (*persona*) to the three members of the Godhead, and, as a consequence, the dogma of

the Trinity as we now know it. Its complete acceptance is marked by the additions to the creed
in the so-called Nicene form, where the Holy
Ghost is described personally as on a par with
the Father and the Son.

The Trinity as a tenet of orthodoxy was
settled pretty early in the third century, but
the Greek mind did not really assimilate it for a
hundred years and more, and then only with
reluctance and under protest. The truth of the
matter is that the leading theologians even of
the fourth century, while constant in their use of
a trinitarian formula, approached the dogma of
the third person with hesitation and never felt
quite sure of their ground.

Thus, no one, I think, can read such passages in Athanasius as chapters 43 to 47 of the
first *Oration against the Arians* without perceiving that to the instinctive feeling of that
great champion of orthodoxy the Holy Ghost
was still not a separate person but the spirit of
God operating through grace and sanctifying
the heart of man. In his *Theological Orations*
on the Trinity Gregory of Nazianzus admits
freely the fluctuating opinions that have prevailed among Christians in regard to the Holy
Ghost, and deals gently with those who hold it

to be merely the "energy" of God, though he leaves no doubt of the regularity of his own position. Basil, the master mind of the Cappadocians, writes his treatise on the subject only under pressure to free himself from charges of heresy; he too is strong on the full divinity of the Spirit (as indeed might be one who held it an impersonal energy), while passing lightly over the question of its, or his, hypostatic independence. In all of these men we can observe two really irreconcilable attitudes: on the one hand, when debating controversially with heretics, they argue for the trinitarian dogma in a fully developed form; whereas, on the other hand, when the need of discussion is not before them, they speak of the operation of the Holy Ghost in a manner quite consistent with what I have called the trinitarian formula. Gregory Nazianzen, preaching on the day of Pentecost, is content to describe the Holy Ghost as "the spirit of adoption, of truth, of wisdom, . . . through which (or whom) the Father is known and the Son is glorified."[6] And in his very oration on the Trinity, in reply to the question what authority we have for worshipping the Spirit, he declares that "it will be enough to say

[6] *Or.*, xli, 9.

this: the Spirit is that in which we worship and
through which we pray; for God, it is said, is
spirit."[7] In the same manner the other Gregory,
Basil's brother, represents the "grace of the
spirit," not as a person, but as the divine work
in the process of salvation corresponding to the
work of justice on the part of man, and de-
scribes the spirit as the finger of God which
writes the tablet of the Law and as the mystic
guidance which reveals to the initiate that which
is invisible to others.[8]

A good deal of what I have said in regard to
the Trinity would be acceptable to the most
sensitive orthodoxy. Thus Dr. Gore, for the
Anglican community, admits that Justin Martyr "seems to confuse the Holy Spirit with the
eternal spiritual being of our Lord";[9] and Tix-
eront, for the Roman Church, virtually con-
cedes that Hippolytus did not reckon the Holy
Ghost a person but "counted two persons in
God, and the grace of the Holy Spirit as third
by 'economy'."[10] But these orthodox historians

[7] *Theol. Or.*, v, 12.
[8] *De Instituto Christiano*, 289 (Migne); *In Laudem Fratris
Basilii*, 812. The regular formula, Ἡ χάρις τοῦ ἁγίου Πνεύματος,
thus means, not "the grace from the Holy Ghost," but "the
grace which is the Holy Ghost," *i.e.* ἡ θεία δύναμις, *i.e.* Plato's θεία
μοῖρα.
[9] *Belief in Christ*, 242.
[10] *Histoire des Dogmes*, I, 400. Cf. also p. 255.

would insist that the dogma of the Trinity, though not fully comprehended or formally defined by the early theologians, is implicit in their words, and that it was the proper office of the Church, under the guidance of the Spirit in question, to develop and elucidate the sacred truth. That, obviously, is a thesis not easily settled or even discussed. To me it seems quite plain that the dogma has no justification in the words of Jesus or in Scripture, that it was forced upon the Church by the mythopoeic tendency of the age, and that it introduced needless perplexities into theology. It seems to me equally clear that the rigid personification of the Holy Ghost is at bottom even unchristian, since it tends to conceal the true nature and function of the spirit as the power of God manifesting Himself in the world, and as the voice of God speaking to the spirit of man and so opening a mystic channel of communion between the divine and the human. In this way only is the majesty of the Holy Ghost reverently maintained, and its importance magnified, as that attribute of God whereon the very life of the Church and the validity of true religion hang. So taken, the trinitarian *formula* may be used in worship with a force and mean-

ing which have almost been lost under the sway
of a wrongly schematized theology. So, indeed,
it is actually taken in that magnificent fugue
on the Apostles' Creed, the *Te Deum,* where,
between the full personal homage to God the
Father and to God the Son, the trinitarian
formula is intercalated with marvellous effect:

> The Father, of an infinite Majesty;
> Thine adorable, true, and only Son;
> Also the Holy Ghost, the Comforter.

If my conjecture is right in regard to the
Holy Ghost and the Trinity, it will follow that
the real problem of the Church did not spring
from this source; and certainly history shows
that the serious conflict with heresy lay elsewhere. From the beginning to the end of our
period, for the Greek community at least, the
cause of contention was the one fact of the Incarnation, and to a reader of the annals of the
age the picture that stands before the eye is of
a rock rising in sublime isolation from the
midst of a sea of seething waves and tides. This
is the point. The early Christians inherited the
monotheism of the Old Testament, while the
New Testament forced upon them the acceptance of a duality of persons in the divine nature.
How should they adapt themselves to this ap-

parent contradiction? Now the safe course for
the Church would have been simply to leave
this paradox as an insoluble enigma of faith, to
be believed or rejected as it seemed to be in
conformity with, or in repugnance to, the deepest intuition of our spiritual experience. But to
do this consistently she must have resisted with
unflinching heroism any invasion from the
metaphysical currents flowing about her on
every side. Here the Church failed, in so far as
she compromised with the language of the
schools. The moment she admitted a rationalistic definition of the supreme object of her
worship as an Absolute Unity (an utterly different thing from an unrationalized monotheism), she was in dire straits to maintain her
belief in the personal divinity of Christ as a
reasonable dogma. You may be reasonable
while repudiating the claims of rationalism to
be the final arbiter of truth; you cannot very
comfortably be rationalistic and irrationalistic
at the same time. Against such a position the
heretics could boast a kind of specious consistency. One and all the major heresiarchs, with
whom alone we are concerned, undertook to
rationalize the belief in Christ in such a manner
as to bring it into logical harmony with a

thoroughly monistic theism; though by so doing
they subjected the faith to canons of criticism
which, if carried to their bitter conclusion,
would have destroyed the very fabric of Christianity.

The whole battle of orthodoxy and heresy
thus centres upon a single dogma. But the contention falls into two quite distinct periods corresponding to two aspects of the question, and
our progress through this jungle of contradictions may be lightened by a brief preliminary
survey of the path to be traversed.

The first aspect of the question belongs to the
narrower field of theology: how can we reconcile belief in one God with belief in the Logos
as incarnate in Jesus Christ? Now all Christians, of whatever stamp, believed in the unity
of the divine nature and in a revelation of God
through the Logos; so that the point really at
issue was how to reconcile their monotheism
with acceptance of the Logos as at once both
fully divine and distinctly personal. And the
answers of heresy swerved in contrary direc-
tions as reason endeavoured to escape one or the
other horn of this dilemma. The Sabellians,
holding fast to the absolute unity of God, accepted the *divinity* of the Logos, and accom-

modated these two tenets by regarding the
Logos not as a separate *personality*, but as a
mere name for God's power of operating in a
peculiar manner and to a specific end. At the
other extreme were the Arians, who, also holding fast to the absolute unity of God, accepted
the *personality* of the Logos, but maintained
their position by lowering the Logos to a rank
somewhere intermediate between God and
humanity; they thus virtually denied the *divinity* of Christ.[11] In this way both Sabellians and
Arians squared their theology with the demands of an uncompromising monism, but in
each case at the expense of the Incarnation,
since for neither Sabellian nor Arian was the
incarnate Logos in the full sense of the word
both divine and personal.

Against these twin heresies the first ecumenical council, held at Nicea in 325, made the
categorical assertion that the Logos was God
and therefore truly divine, while at the same
time, as the incarnate Son, it was in some way
distinct from the Father. Henceforth the
Church, though her schoolmen might continue
to speak the language of the monism which had

---

[11] Athanasius could thus, *Cont. Ar.*, I, 40, speak of the ἄλογοι
ἔννοιαι of the Arians.

brought her to the dolorous pass, in dogma and
in the practice of worship was committed to
what may be called a monotheistic dyadism (not
to mention the further and, as I contend, erroneous expansion to trinitarianism).

But no sooner were the theological heresies
crushed than a new difficulty arose in the more
strictly Christological aspect of the problem.
The personal divinity of the Logos is now con-
ceded. Very well; but what of the humanity of
Christ? Tradition taught that the Jesus of history, a person known and loved in the flesh, was,
in some manner not defined, human as well as
divine; how should such a belief be squared with
the demands of consistency? And here again
the way of heresy was to escape the paradox of
faith by throwing itself upon one or the other
horn of the dilemma. The Nestorian answer
was to declare: Certainly there were two natures in Christ, he was both human and divine;
but you cannot rationally have two distinct natures in one person, and therefore there must
have been also two persons (virtually so, at
least) in Jesus. On the other side the Monophysites insisted on the unity of person, and
argued hence that there could not have been
two distinct natures; and as by the Nicene

Faith the divine nature was put beyond cavil, they denied the humanity of Christ. In either case, whether one inclines from the straight path to the Nestorian side of two persons or to the Monophysite side of one nature, it will be seen that, as in the earlier heresies, the full force and meaning of the Incarnation are sacrificed.

Against this second pair of contradictory theories the Church at Chalcedon, in 451, again by a categorical statement which waived the pretensions of rationalism, simply insisted that Christ was one person of two natures.

Without pressing the analogy too far one might elucidate the course of theology by comparing it with that of secular philosophy. The latter, for our purpose, began with Socrates, who in his life and doctrine stood for a spontaneous and undefined dualism: on the one side his hedonism and endurance (*karteria*), and on the other side his spiritual affirmation.[12] Then came the rationalizing schools of Epicurus and Zeno, who developed the Socratic hedonism and endurance each into a thoroughgoing monism, and of Plotinus, who erected the spiritual affirmation into an equally rigid mon-

12 For a detailed exposition of this thesis I may refer to *Hellenistic Philosophies*, particularly Appendix B.

ism. Meanwhile Plato had worked out the naïve doctrine of his master into a complete philosophy of dualism. For one who examines with open mind the course of these various schools the notable point is that Plato, by conceding paradox in the nature of things as known to human experience, was able to construct a consistent and reasonable philosophy, whereas the monists, by rejecting that paradox in the name of reason, ran into a variety of metaphysical theories which not only falsified the facts of life, but also were contradictory with one another and inconsistent each within itself.

It should seem therefore that our only choice lies between a reasonable philosophy based on an irrational paradox and an unreasonable metaphysic based on a rational presumption. And I cannot see how the like alternative can be avoided in the attitude we take towards the contending claims of an orthodox philosophy and an heretical metaphysic in the dogmas of religion. The parallel may be presented to the eye schematically as follows, with the proviso, however, that it aims only at a rough approximation to the facts:

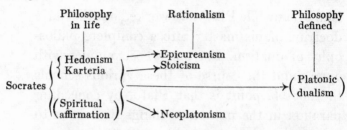

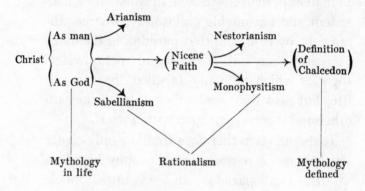

CHAPTER V

SABELLIANISM AND ARIANISM

WRITING to the authorities of Neocaesarea in the mid-fourth century St. Basil groans in spirit because he is obliged, like a man engaged with two boxers at once, to defend the truth against the contrary attacks of Arians and Sabellians.[1] And in his *Orations* Athanasius is constantly aware of the same duplicity of error, though with him one enemy seems far more urgent than the other. The situation has a curious resemblance to the ancient feud of gods and giants in philosophy over the nature of Being, between whose embattled ranks Plato found himself placed as a much buffeted mediator,—on the one side the overzealous idealists who would strip the divine reality of all relation to human life and leave it suspended in solemn vacuity, and on the other side the materialists who would drag all things down from heaven

[1] *Epist.*, ccx (Migne 773A).

and would believe only what they could see and feel and define.[2]

Of the two heresies that of Sabellius was the older, having its roots indeed in the docetism which had brought dismay to the Apostolic Church. The particular occasion of its rise was the spread of Gnosticism, and its special form was determined by the force of reaction. Against the gnostic tendency to split up the divine Pleroma into a group of Aeons, it was natural that the Christians should stress the monarchical unity of their God. In this way the term monarchianism came to be used as a philosophical equivalent for monotheism in the orthodox revolt against a virtual polytheism. That was well, the word was plausible and reasonable, and might throw confusion into the camp of the enemy; but those who took it up incautiously did not see at first the danger also it imported into their own camp. It might scatter the Aeons of Valentine and bring discredit on the theistic dualism of Marcion, but in so doing what place would it leave for their own irrational divinity of the Logos? Having appealed to reason should not the Christian abide

---

[2] *Sophist,* 246Aff. Athanasius, *Contra Ar.,* ii, 32, has a clear reference to this "gigantomachy," and Clement, *Strom.,* II, iv, 15, quotes the text, though they both rather miss Plato's point.

by its decisions to the end? So it happened that Monarchianism became the catchword for those heretics who, under the pressure of logic, went beyond the reasonable defence of the faith and denied any independent existence to the Logos, merging together Father and Son in the conception of indivisible, impersonal, all-embracing deity: at any cost they would have one God, not two. The old story is repeated: flying from one extreme the human mind rushes into the other extreme, escaping polytheism it falls into monism.

So long as these monists soared in the altitude of pure theology they met with no serious obstacle, but the moment they descended to earth and sought to explain how the Word was embodied in Jesus Christ, they found it not so easy to be logical. Faced with the question raised by the Incarnation Monarchianism took many forms, showing the Protean variability common to all heresy. In the main, however, these early sectaries may be divided into two groups, according as they verge more to a pantheistic view of the divine economy or to emanation. Technically the former group is known to scholars as the modalistic, while the second staggers under the title of dynamistic Monarch-

ians, portentous names, one must admit, but
concealing a fairly simple idea.

The great champion of the modalistic form
of the heresy was Sabellius, a native of the
Lybian Pentapolis, who taught in Rome some
time about the year 220. The gist of his doctrine
was that God, as a pure monad, essentially immutable, manifested Himself in various modes,
first as Father in the act of creation and legisla-
tion, then as Son in the task of redemption, and
lastly as Holy Ghost in the operation of grace.
And these successive manifestations are further
explained as a mere process of expansion or extension of the divine substance, in such a manner that, passing into the world, God becomes
the world, and the act of creation is reduced to
a kind of pantheistic illusion.

More figuratively expressed, the divine appearances are masks[3] assumed by God as He
plays one part or the other in the grand drama
of the economy, while behind the disguise He
abides the same unchanging entity. He is called
Father *non quia genuit, sed quia condidit*; and
when called Son He is so far from bearing a

[3] *Prosôpa.* It is one of the curious and perplexing facts of theology, that this word, in its fuller sense of "persons," was employed by the Greeks, following the Latin usage of *personae*
introduced by Tertullian, to distinguish the three hypostases
of the Godhead.

filial relation to another person that the truer designation for Him is not Father and Son but conjointly Son-Father. Even this distinction of names Sabellius seems to have admitted only to avoid the hated charge of patripassianism, which held the Monarchians to the inconsistency of teaching that God the Father was immutable and impassible, yet simply as God suffered the ignominy of crucifixion. But the escape from that dilemma was merely nominal, so long as behind the names of Father and Son there was no corresponding individuality of persons. Effectually the Sabellians could avoid the patripassian abomination only by way of the more disastrous error of docetism, by holding, that is to say, that the Logos, whether Father or Son, did not in any honest sense of the word become flesh, and took no real part in the life of the man Jesus.[4] In fact the moment Sabellius brought his theological dream into contact with

---

[4] It is fair to say that there is no middle ground between docetism and patripassianism. That is, if the Son really suffered then the Father must have suffered with him. Tertullian, in his attack on Praxeas, a Monarchian before Sabellius, states the case for orthodoxy as well as it can be put (*Contra Prax.*, ii); but any such distinction as will avoid patripassianism fades away before the great text, "God so loved the world that he gave his only begotten Son." In general orthodox theology, enslaved to its metaphysical conception of deity, lays the suffering of Jesus to his human nature while his divine nature remains impassive. But this at bottom is all that docetism meant to say.

the human drama of the Gospel, it broke itself on the inner contradiction that lurks in the logic of all would-be pantheistic philosophies.

Sabellius, though his doctrine has come down to us in the most fragmentary shape, was important enough to overshadow all his predecessors, and to give his name to the whole group of heresies. In Athanasius, for instance, Sabellianism and Monarchianism are equivalent terms. Yet a far greater representative of the school, a portentous figure of Church history, is Paul of Samosata, who, though himself a Monarchian, yet by the peculiar turn given to the doctrine became the forefather of the great heresies of Arius and Nestorius, who, as our diagram has shown, made their attack from an apparently opposite point of view. And this, as was remarked more than once by the Fathers, forms a characteristic mark of heresy, that the various sects, even though seemingly contradictory, had a way of gliding one into the other, owing to their common origin in the attempt to rationalize theology on a monistic basis. We have seen the same thing happen in philosophical sects as hostile to each other as Epicureanism and Stoicism, and for the same reason.[5]

5 *Hellenistic Philosophies,* 28 *et al.*

Paul was born in the royal town of Syria.
For a while he lived under the protection of
Zenobia, the romantic queen of the little empire within the Roman world, with its capital
at Palmyra. For about twelve years, *c.* 260-272,
he was bishop of Antioch, and at the same time
held high secular office with a large salary. He
lived in magnificent state, with throngs of at-
tendants, had his throne and *secretum* in the
Church like a civil magistrate, and in general
created the type of princely ecclesiastics, not
without suspicion of scandalous irregularities.
Owing to his influence with Zenobia he maintained his position against repeated synodal
censure; in 269 he was excommunicated, but
still clung to his house and living until after the
fall of the queen.

As a heretic Paul belonged to what is called
the dynamistic branch of the Monarchians, as
distinguished from the modalistic school of Sabellius. That is to say, he insisted like all the
Monarchians on the absolute undivided unity
of the Godhead, but instead of explaining the
divine economy by the various modes of God's
self-manifestation, now as Father and then as
Son, or Logos, and Holy Ghost, he thought of
the Logos as a constant faculty, or attribute

(*dynamis*), of God. He would admit that the Word might be regarded as eternally begotten, and so in a manner as the Son; but it still remained, like the reason and speech of man, impersonal, a mere faculty of the unchanging cause, and no true hypostasis. So far his doctrine is purely monarchian; when he comes to the question of the Incarnation his dynamism is, as it were, doubled—I beg the lay reader not to be dismayed by this array of barbarous names—with adoptionism. That is to say, Paul held that Christ was not both God and man by nature and birth, as the orthodox believed, nor veritable God, the Son-Father, while only appearing to be man, as Sabellius taught, but a true man who was raised to divinity by adoption. The procedure was as follows. Jesus, though born of a virgin (an unexpected concession doubtless to the Gospel story), was of purely human origin. At some time in his life, whether at birth or at baptism, the Word, which aforetime had spoken through the prophets, descended upon him in a peculiar manner, dwelling within him as in a temple, yet not essentially nor as a person, but as a divine attribute. Drawn by this power (*dynamis*) Jesus grew in grace and progressed always towards

higher things, performing miracles, triumphing over sin in himself and in other men, until
his will became one with God's will, and his
union with deity was so compacted as to be in-
dissoluble. In view of this ultimate sonship
Paul would speak of Jesus proleptically as
"God born of a virgin and God manifest in
Nazareth," and figuratively as "preëxistent";
but withal he was Son only by adoption, not by
the inalienable right of his nature.

By this theory of Jesus as the adopted Son,
the next school of theology we have to study
may be traced from Paul, through Lucian of
Antioch, who apparently combined the Monarchianism of Paul with some form of Origen's
doctrine of the subordinate personality of the
Son, to Lucian's pupil, Arius, the great heresi-
arch of Alexandria. Again we see an attempt to
save the absolute unity of God by raising Him
into an infinite isolation from the world; but
now the Incarnation will be explained, not by
taking the Logos as a mere mode of God's
being or as an attribute of God, but as an intermediate power between God and man, neither
quite Creator nor quite creature, who enters
into union with the man Jesus and raises him by
adoption to Sonship as, so to speak, a quasi

deity. If orthodox Christianity may be described as an interpretation of the claims of Jesus in terms of the philosophy of Plato, the theology of the Alexandrian heresy may be set against it as the most complete amalgamation of the Christian myth with the current of Neoplatonic monism tempered by intermediaries, which in its essential thesis goes back to Aristotle.

In his private life Arius was without reproach; as a preacher he was eloquent and persuasive, perhaps a little inclined to trade on his popularity. At any rate he soon made himself notorious by the peculiar trend of his doctrine. At first Alexander, then Bishop of Alexandria, was conciliatory and tried private remonstrance; but Arius was stubborn, and in 321 a synod of local bishops deposed him from his office as presbyter. Arius then withdrew from Egypt to Syria and Asia, where he excited the sympathy of various important leaders of the Church, particularly of Eusebius of Nicomedia, at that time the eastern capital of the Empire. What had started as an insignificant squabble began to assume the proportions of a wide-spread rebellion. Put upon the defensive, Alexander sent out several letters of apology and protest, the first and most important of which was an Encyclical, signed by thirty-four priests and forty-four deacons. This document, a clear and forceful statement of the circumstances and of the question at issue, bears evidence of the hand of Athanasius, then a young deacon in the household of the bishop, and is included in his works. It "contains the germ of which his whole series of anti-Arian writings are the expansion."

The works of Arius have been swept away with the vast body of heretical books by the torrent of orthodoxy, and if sometimes in the interest of historical accuracy we should like to have a view of that Augean stable before it was cleansed, I think on the whole we have been spared more than we have lost. The student of that age finds the literature voluminous enough in all conscience. Nor in the case of Arius can there be any doubt as to the main purport of his teaching. Among his writings was a poem entitled *Thalia,* composed in the Sotadean measure employed ordinarily for the most frivolous and obscene subjects. The gist of the poem can be gathered from the quotations given by Athanasius.

"Not always was God a father, but there was when God was alone and was not yet a father. . . . Not always was the Son; for all things having come into being from what was not, . . . so the Logos himself of God came into being from what was not, and there was when he was not. And he was not before he came into being, but himself also had a beginning in creation. . . . Wishing thereafter to create us, He (God) then made a certain one, and named him Logos and Wisdom and Son, in order that through him He might create us. For there are two Wisdoms, one His own and coexistent with God, and in this Wisdom the Son was made, and as partaking thereof was merely named Wisdom and Logos. . . . There is thus another Logos besides the Son in God, by participation whereof the Son himself is named secondarily by grace Logos and Son. . . . There are many powers (*dynameis*), and the one belongs to God by nature and is eternal, whereas Christ on the other hand is not a true power of God but one of the so-called powers. . . . And in nature the Logos also, like all others, is subject to change, though by his own free will he remains good (*kalos*) so long as he wishes; but when he wishes, he can change, he also, like us, being of a changeable nature. Wherefore God, foreknowing that he would be good, gave him by anticipation this glory which as man and by reason of his virtue he afterwards had. So that by reason of his deeds, which God foreknew, He caused him to be made as he now is. . . . Neither is the Logos true God, and if he is called God, yet is he not so in truth, but by participation of grace he, like all others, is merely called God by name."[6]

But poems and sermons were not the only method employed to catch the people. Athanasius declares that emissaries of the heresy waylaid young children in the market place with puzzling problems such as this: "Did He-who-is create him-who-is-not, or did He create him-who-is from that-which-is-not?"—and bewildered ignorant women with such questions as "Whether they had a son before they gave birth?" A strange alliance of metaphysics and buffoonery that set the tongues of the world wagging to the detriment of faith and decency. Gregory of Nyssa complains that, in his part of the world, "if you ask the price of a loaf, you are told that the Son is subject to the Father; if you ask whether a bath is ready, the answer is that the Son was made out of nothing."

Meanwhile, amidst this hubbub of tongues, illiterate and learned, a new force was entering upon the stage. In the year 313 Constantine and Licinius issued their famous edict at Milan,

[6] *Contra Ar.,* i, 5 and 6.

whereby free and absolute power was given to Christians, and to all others, to worship as each individual chose for himself, and strict orders were laid upon the governors of the provinces to secure unlimited religious liberty. It is not within the plan of this book to consider the steps by which Constantine became converted to Christianity or to discuss the sincerity of his change, but the event itself was of vast significance. In 312 Maximin in the East was submitting the Church to organized and bloody persecution, directed mainly against the bishops and theologians. In April of the next year, one month after the Edict of Milan, he suffered defeat by Licinius at Adrianople, and in twenty-four hours fled to Nicomedia, a distance of one hundred and sixty miles; from there he proceeded to Tarsus, where he died, it is said, of delirium tremens. In 319 Licinius, having broken with Constantine, subjected the Christian population of the East to annoying hardships, hoping thereby to win the support of the Pagans in his struggle for the Empire. In 323 he was besieged by Constantine in Byzantium, escaped across the Bosphorus, and there suffered the defeat which left his rival sole master of the world. The next year Constantine sent out circular letters exhorting all his subjects to imitate their Emperor in accepting the divine truth which had given him victory over his enemies. Christianity henceforth, except for the brief interval under Julian, was the recognized Church of the State, though at the time of its establishment it still probably counted a minority of the subjects. The world has perhaps seen no other such revolution as that which occurred in the twelve years between the persecutions of Maximin and the circular letters of Constantine.

Meanwhile, in these very years, the new religion which Constantine had embraced, partly if not primarily, as an imperial instrument of pacification and unification, was showing anything but peace and unity within itself. The leading bishops of the East were divided into hostile camps over the new question of Arianism, not to mention the relics of older Sabellian heresies, and the very marketplaces of the towns had been converted into centres of theological wrangling. The first move of the Emperor was to send his confidential adviser, Hosius Bishop of Cordova, to Alexandria with a letter addressed to both Alexander and Arius, imploring them for the good of the Empire to lay aside their differences over a quibble that did not affect the faith. "It was not decent," he says, "ever to have inquired concerning such matters, or to answer if questioned. For these investigations which are forced upon us by no necessity of the law and are rather the fruit of a vain and disputatious idleness, even if they have some profit in the exercise of our natural faculties, ought to be locked within the breast, and not brought forward lightly in public synods or intrusted carelessly to the hearing of the people." On the surface the plea of the Emperor sounds like an echo of the constant complaint of the Church that these mysteries of religion should never have been laid before the incompetent court of reason; but in effect the well-meant interference of Constantine only embroiled matters further, because he failed to see that the initiative in the evil lay with the heretics and not with both parties equally, and that such questions when once raised could not be shirked as mere quibbles.

The next step of the Emperor was to summon a general council where the point at issue might be settled and some canon of orthodoxy might be established once for all. To this end the town of Nicea in Bithynia was chosen, and

thither, in the early summer of 325, the leading
bishops of the East with a few from the West
came together in solemn conclave. Synods had
been held before this in various places and for
various purposes, but this was the first world,
or "ecumenical," council, and its authority has
always been acknowledged by all branches of
the Church as supreme and indisputable.
"You," said Constantine, who took part in the
meeting but with ostentatious humility as an
outsider,—"you," he said to the bishops, "are
in charge of the internal affairs of the Church;
I am appointed by God to be bishop of her relations to the world at large."

Of the detailed proceedings of the council
not much is known; and this perhaps is just as
well, for the spirit of intrigue and violence
showed itself here, as it did in larger measure
on other occasions of the sort. The first move
towards a settlement apparently came from the
Arians, when Eusebius of Nicomedia introduced a formulary for adoption, only to see it
indignantly torn up in the presence of all as
heretical. Then his namesake of Caesarea, the
most learned of the bishops, but a waverer between Arianism and conservatism, neither of
which he clearly comprehended, offered the

baptismal creed of his own church, as follows:

"We believe in one God, Father Almighty, the maker of all things visible and invisible; and in one Lord Jesus Christ, the Word (Logos) of God, God of God, Light of Light, Life of Life, only-begotten Son, first-born of all creation, begotten of his Father before all ages, through whom also all things were made, who for our salvation was made (became) flesh and lived among men, and suffered, and rose again on the third day, and ascended to the Father, and will come again in glory to judge the quick and the dead. We believe also in one Holy Ghost,—believing that each of these is and subsists: the Father truly Father, the Son truly Son, the Holy Ghost truly Holy Ghost; as our Lord also said, when he sent his disciples to preach: Go teach all nations, baptizing them in the name of the Father and of the Son and of the Holy Ghost."

After some debate Constantine, at a suggestion probably of Hosius, proposed that this creed should be accepted, "with the addition of a single word *homoousios*," and to this proposal the assembly agreed. So Eusebius himself tells the story; but as a matter of fact the Faith as it was finally adopted and signed differs in more than a word from the Eusebian creed. It reads as follows:

"We believe in one God, Father Almighty, maker of all things visible and invisible; and in one Lord Jesus Christ, the Son of God, begotten of the Father, only-begotten, who is of the substance (*ousia*) of the Father, God of God, Light of Light, very God of very God, begotten, not made, of one substance (*homoousios*) with the Father, through whom all things were made, both things in heaven and things in earth, who for us men and for our salvation came down and was made (became) flesh and was made (became) man, suffered, and rose again the third day, ascended into heaven, and cometh to judge the quick and the dead.

"And in the Holy Ghost.

"But those who say there was when he was not, and before being begotten he was not, and he was made out of things that were not, or those who say that the Son of God was from a different substance (*hypostasis*) or essence (*ousia*), or a creature, or capable of change or alteration, these the Catholic Church anathematizes."

Now the question immediately arises, why the Faith, as promulgated at Nicea, differed so widely from the creed proposed by Eusebius of Caeserea. And to this question, so far as the additions are concerned, there is a ready answer: the council found the Eusebian creed not

sufficiently explicit in regard to the complete
undifferentiated divinity of Christ. On this
point no uncertainty, no loophole of evasion,
should be left for those who affixed their signa-
tures. But in regard to the omissions the answer
is not so easy. It will be observed that in the
creed, which was rejected, or modified, the trinitarian formula from Matt. xxviii, 19 is developed into a succinct dogma of the Trinity,
whereas in the Faith the Holy Ghost is indeed
mentioned, but not in such a manner as to en-
force the belief in a third person. Of the fact
that the assembled Fathers at that time actually
believed in the Trinity there can be no doubt,
and their omission of the trinitarian clause can
only be explained, I think, by the supposition
that the importance of the divinity of Christ so
overshadowed in their minds all other matters
of faith as to make a distinction between this
dogma, which should be the fundamental crite-
rion of orthodoxy, and other dogmas, which
should be left as in a way secondary, neither
sharply defined nor necessarily subscribed. At
any rate this was the effect of the transaction,
whatever the motive may have been; from that
day to this the Faith of Nicea has remained the
final test of orthodoxy; Christianity is cotermi-

nous with a full and unequivocal acceptance of the Incarnation, with its single antecedent, belief in God the Father and Creator, and its essential corollary, belief in the resurrection and in the communion of God through the spirit.

CHAPTER VI

THE ARIAN SECTS

THE immediate outcome of the Council of Nicea was a complete victory for the contention of Alexander and his young deacon, Athanasius, and for the imperial desire for unity. The formula of the Faith was signed by all but five of the three hundred and eighteen members (such is the traditional number), and the few recalcitrants, with Arius himself, were sent into exile by the Emperor. But the triumph, if brilliant, was short-lived. In a little while Eusebius of Nicomedia, the statesman of the Arian party, was back at his post, and had won the ear of the court. The mischief of calling in the State as virtual arbiter in matters of faith soon became apparent under the wavering policy of Constantine, and under his successor Constantius, who inclined openly to the Arian wing, very nearly resulted in tragedy. Heresy flourished and multiplied, until in a short time the ortho-

dox party, who boasted that they were called
by the name of no man but were simply the
Church, the *Ekklêsia*, found itself in opposition
to an interminable spawn of sects, who agreed
only in this, that they had no taste for the formula pronounced at Nicea.

Amid the welter of these factions, three main
groups can be distinguished by their attitude
towards the prickly central word of the Faith.
Closest to the orthodox minority were the so-
called semi-Arians, whose tongues would not
say *homo-ousios,* "of one substance," or "of the
same substance," but found no difficulty in
gliding over *homoi-ousios,* "of like substance."
In the end these semi-Arians, whose quarrel
with the formula, as Athanasius pointed out,
was really more verbal than doctrinal, coalesced
by mutual concessions with the Church and were
sharers in the final victory; but for a time it
looked as though the world were to be broken
asunder over an iota. As Gibbon, with his solemn sneer, declares: "The profane of every age
have derided the furious contests which the difference of a single diphthong excited between
the Homoousians and the Homoiousians."

Below these semi-Arians, who in fact were
largely conservatives rather than heretics, came

a second group known as Acacians, from their leader Acacius, or as Homoeans, who objected on philosophical and biblical grounds to the use of the term *ousia* (substance, or essence) in the creed, but were quite ready to admit that otherwise the Son was "in all things like" (*homoios kata panta*) to the Father. In their contest with the Niceans they showed the slipperiness of the serpent, devising formula after formula which reproduced the ideas of the Nicene Faith, barring always the fatal shibboleth of the word *homoousios*. Apart from the verbal difference there was undoubtedly in most of these rebels a hesitation to admit the full and undifferentiated divinity of Christ, and in some of them the phrase "in all things like" was a dishonest subterfuge, adopted because it might pass as an equivalent for *homoousios* yet secretly could be applied to the divine element in Christ as a creature in the sense that man also was made in the likeness of God. It was this ambiguity that made the Homoeans the most dangerous enemies of the Church, since on the one hand they could satisfy all but the intransigent of the Arians, while on the other hand they could lay the onus of schism on the orthodox party. "Was it right," they could ask the sticklers for the word *ousia,* "to stand out so stiffly for it, when, the moment it was surrendered, divisions would be at an end? All that was wanted was to say simply that the Son is like the Father." Or: "Is it Christianity you want, or only a formula? Which do you worship—Christ or the *homoousios?*"

These two parties, the semi-Arians and the Homoeans, were essentially compromisers, ranging up and down within the penumbra of linguistic confusion. The true followers of Arius were the so-called Anomoeans (from *anomoios,* "unlike"), who carried the motive of the heresy to its logical conclusion. They were at least honest. To them God, in the language of the schools, was absolute being, absolutely one and simple. By reason of His simplicity (as a pure abstraction of reason) He is perfectly comprehensible to reason, and Eunomius, the most philosophical of the party leaders, could say unblushingly, "I know God as well as He knows himself." By reason of His unity as absolute being, God could have no one in any way like Him or a participant of His nature. In particular, they laid stress on the fact that as supreme cause it was of God's very essence to be ungenerated, or unbegotten (*agennêtos*), so that anything begotten must be essentially different from God in the same manner that all created things are different. Hence Christ, the Son, may indeed rank first among created things by reason of the primacy of his creation, he may by his moral superiority stand as an intermediary between God and man; he is withal, as generated or begotten, of a different essence and nature from God, and in this sense not *homoousios*, nor yet even "like."

These were the three main divisions of the heresy that sprang from a local disagreement in the Alexandrian Church, lost itself for a moment at Nicea, and then grew and swelled until it threatened to submerge the world. But within and between and about these divisions there were countless shades of opinion and constant changes of adherence, so that the historian Socrates could speak of the "labyrinth" of the Arian sects and Ambrose could ridicule their "multifarious incoherencies." Between the Council of Nicea and the year 361 it is calculated that the various parties put out twenty different creeds;—as numerous a brood as the serpents of Pharaoh's wise men and sorcerers that were swallowed up by the rod of Aaron.

To one who reads the history of that age

superficially it may seem as if the world had gone mad over a mere word. What was this vocable *homoousios,* that it should arouse such fury of protest and such heroism of devotion, sending men into exile and threatening to deluge the State with blood? There can be no doubt that, after its first unreflecting acceptance at Nicea, it brought dismay to many who were perfectly loyal to the traditional belief, and was the cause of division among those who at heart were in unison. And unquestionably there were solid reasons for objecting to its interjection into the creed as a shibboleth of orthodoxy. Many of conservative habit disliked the very sound of the word *ousia,* because it was unscriptural (*agraphon*) and seemed to introduce the vexatious subtleties of philosophy into the simplicity of faith. Others were frightened because it came with the taint of former heresies upon it. Thus Sabellius had used *ousia* for person, so that *homoousios* would imply that the Son was not a separate personality from the Father, and the Nicene Faith would thus save the Church from the error of Arius only by thrusting it back into Sabellianism. Again, the use of the term had been condemned at the Synod of Antioch in 269 as in some way (not clear to us as the records stand) connected with the teaching of Paul of Samosata who was the forerunner of Arius, so that its revival might seem to countenance the very heresy it was intended to check.

These were honest objections, which caused the champions of the Faith no light embarrassment as may be seen in the repeated efforts of Athanasius to answer them. But I think a candid student must admit also that no better term could have been devised for the occasion, and that in the end it proved to be the salvation of the Church and of Christianity. In the first place it should be understood that the term *homoousios,* notwithstanding its colour of abstraction, was not coined, or resuscitated, for the purpose of enforcing a metaphysical subtlety, but on the contrary was meant to be a bulwark against such an encroachment on the simplicity of religion. The first letter of Alexander (or Athanasius?), written after the expulsion of Arius from Alexandria, shows quite clearly in what spirit the Fathers met together at Nicea: they were there to protest against the strange and unscriptural novelties of those who lifted the conception of Deity so high into the empyrean of reason as to render Him ineffable and incomprehensible even to the Son; they perceived that if such a conception prevailed there could be no true revelation of God as a person, while in our homage to Christ we should be worshipping only a variable and mutable creature like ourselves. It may be that the Church, by its own incautious excursions into a transcendental theology, had opened the door to just these heresies; nevertheless in their contention with Arianism the Fathers were not rationalizing, but protesting, in the spirit of true religion, against a rationalism which emptied the world of God. There are stories of the council which, whether apocryphal or authentic, leave no doubt of this anti-metaphysical bias. On one occasion, when certain theologians were "attempting to fly into the secrets of the deity on the waxen wings of the reason," they were called to their senses by a simple layman, blinded and maimed in the persecution, with the rebuke: "Christ and the Apostles left us not a system of logic, nor a vain deceit, but the naked truth, to be guarded by faith and good works." And on another occasion a loquacious disputant was silenced by a bishop with the words: "Dear friend, we have already told you once for all that in questions of divine mysteries you should never ask the *wherefore* or the *how*."

So we find Athanasius repeatedly in his debate with the Arians dwelling on the fact that the relation between Father and Son is not to be subjected to the rational categories of time and space. The eternal generation of the Son is not so much a metaphysical theorem of timelessness as an expression of a mystical kinship which surpasses our comprehension; whereas all those temporal phrases such as "before the aeons" and "there was when he was not," by which Arius sought to salve the divine event for reason by referring to it a time before the beginning of time, explain nothing and only end in logical confusion.[1] Again, in regard to the proximity of the two persons, it is not to be supposed that one is locally in the other, or that something passes between them as when one empty vessel is filled from another; nor are their unity and separation such as can be illustrated by the combination and division of an extended material body. Rather the word sonship indicates the qualitative connexion of two persons who are distinct yet have in all things the same nature and will, while the epithet

[1] *E.g. Contra Ar.*, i, 11; *Ep. ad Monachos*, 16.

Logos applied to the Son shows that there is a simple divine purpose (*pronoia*) unfolding itself in the economy of the world. Above all the insistence on the complete and consubstantial divinity of Christ does not spring from any ontological consideration of being or substance (*ousia*) as such, but looks to the end that our worship of God may be real and single. It means that, in lifting our hearts to the divine as revealed by Jesus Christ, we do homage neither to a vague intermediary power between God and man after the fashion of the philosophers, nor to two Gods after the manner of the heathen —for in their nature, *i.e.* their Godhead, Father and Son are the same, however they subsist separately in some personal relation.[2]

It is not Athanasius alone who protests against the usurpations of reason and false logic; this is the constant position of the Fathers. Gregory of Nazianzus, for instance, devoted the whole of one of his orations (*De Moderatione in Disputando*) to a plea for the simplicity of faith as contrasted with the idle

[2] *Contra Ar.*, iii, 1 ff.; iii, 11; *De Synod.*, 34. In his treatise *Adv. Macedonios* (§§ 8, 9, *et al.*) Gregory of Nyssa shows that it is impossible to speak of more or less honour when once the character of deity is granted. Gregory is here writing about the Holy Ghost, but his argument applies equally well to the Arian treatment of the Logos.

curiosity and vain disputatiousness of heresy.
His friend and namesake of Nyssa rebuked the
schismatics for their presumption in supposing
that they could comprehend the secret of deity,
thereby showing themselves more foolish than
the Athenians who set up an altar to the Unknown God.[3] Theodoret declares that it is the
devil himself who, taking advantage of man's
pride of intellect, disturbed the humble trust of
believers with the sophistries of Greece.[4] And
Hilary laments that "the blasphemies of heresy
have forced the Church to deal with unlawful
matters, to scale perilous heights, to speak
things unutterable, to trespass on forbidden
ground. Faith ought in silence to fulfil the commandments, worshipping the Father, rever-
encing with Him the Son, abounding in the
Holy Ghost. . . . But by vice not our own we
are driven into vice, daring thus to embody in
human terms truths which ought to be hidden
in the silent veneration of the heart."[5] And
though the Church too often in later years forgot her mission so far as to lend her authority
to more than one high-blown fabric of rational-

---

[3] *De Deitate Filii*, 537cd (Migne).
[4] *Haeret. Fab.*, 433A: Τὸ ἁπλοῦν καὶ ἀτεχνολόγητον τῆς πίστεως ἡμῶν
ἑλληνικοῖς συνταράττων σοφίσμασι.
[5] *De Trin.*, ii, 2.

ism, yet the old cry of protest is heard again and again. The true authors of the Council of Trent and of its elaborate definitions, says Joseph de Maistre, most intransigent of Ultramontanes, were Luther and Calvin. "The faith would be a thousand times more angelic if a sophistical opposition had not forced it to write: it weeps over the decisions which revolt dragged from it, and which were always misfortunes, since they all suppose doubt or attack."[6]

Negatively the fateful term *homoousios* could be defended as in no sense designed to be metaphysical, though it might be unscriptural; positively it had the great merit of furnishing, in this weltering warfare where friend and foe were often hard to distinguish, a clear battle-cry about which the faithful could rally, and which could not by any device of double reading or sly construction or silent "reservation" be

[6] Quoted by James Stephens, *Horae Sabbaticae,* III, 290.—There is no inconsistency in the Arian theories that God can be known absolutely and that He is incomprehensible even to the Son. The knowledge of which, for example, Eunomius boasted means that Deity has been rationalized to pure Being without content. Such an abstraction can be expressed ontologically like a mathematical equation, but it contains nothing comprehensible. The orthodox position is that the ultimate nature of God is inexpressible but that it is rich in qualities humanly comprehensible. The Church in her long history cannot be cleared of the charge of obscurantism, but this rejection of a rationalizing metaphysic is not of that order; it is compatible with a profound philosophy of religion.

perverted to the service of heresy. This was understood by Arians of all grades, from the well-meaning and muddle-headed Eusebius of Caesarea to the very clear-headed and malignant Eusebius of Nicomedia; hence the unanimity of attack.

It is a constant reproach in the mouth of Athanasius that those who seek a new creed are left to drift through endless changes of opinion, and can never be at rest until they return once more to the Nicene Faith. "See," he exclaims, "what becomes of those who desert that standing ground! They are carried about with every blast of doctrine: council following on council, and symbol superseding symbol, are evidences of their doom of instability." Nor was this the only penalty of abandoning the traditional faith for views more satisfactory to the individual reason; in that instability there was inevitably a downward tendency. Between the one fixed point of admitting the full Godhead of Christ and the fixed point of regarding him as man and only man, that is, between the superrational point at the one extreme and the rationalistic point at the other extreme, there is not only no firm ground to stand on, but just so sure as the mind undertakes to discover and de-

fine some intermediary station where reason
and faith may be reconciled, just so surely
will reason gradually prevail until nothing is
left of the original faith but a pure humanitarianism. We may revolt against this alternative
—the bulk of the Arians did rebel against it in
antiquity, as do the "liberal theologians" today
—but history proves it to be unavoidable. As a
consequence, it must be said that the champions
of the Nicene Faith were contending not for
their own shade of belief against a slightly different shade; they saw that in this contention
Christianity itself as a religion was at stake. If,
by ill chance, any sect of the Arians had been
victorious, even the semi-Arians who seemed
orthodox in all but a question of terminology,
Christianity would have sunk with the general
débâcle of antiquity. It is inconceivable that a
humanitarian religion should have conquered
the world; and this truth has been recognized
by critics of history, such as Gibbon and J. R.
Green, who approached the question certainly
with no bias in favour of orthodoxy. Carlyle,
from his detestation of sham rationalism and
half-sincerities, could say bluntly that, "if the
Arians had won, it (Christianity) would have
dwindled away to a legend"; and Lord Bal-

four, speaking as a philosopher for the present as well as the past, has summed up the whole matter admirably:

"The Church held that all such explanations or partial explanations inflicted irremediable impoverishment on the idea of the Godhead which was essentially involved in the Christian revelation. They insisted on preserving that idea in all its inexplicable fullness; and so it has come about that while such simplifications as those of the Arians, for example, are so alien and impossible to modern modes of thought that if they had been incorporated with Christianity they must have destroyed it, the doctrine of Christ's Divinity still gives reality and life to the worship of millions of pious souls, who are wholly ignorant both of the controversy to which they owe its preservation, and of the technicalities which its discussion has involved."[7]

All this must be remembered when we hear, with some amazement, perhaps, the echoes of those debates, far away and long ago, over that strange word *homoousios* which flames out of the heart of the Nicene Faith. But it should not be forgotten also that behind the Faith stood one of the greatest, one of the most magnificent and dominant personalities in the whole range of history. From his appearance at Nicea as a

[7] *The Foundations of Belief,* 279.

deacon in attendance upon the Bishop of Alexandria, until his death in 373, full of years and in the haven of rest after many storms, a figure already sainted in the eyes of the new generation upon whom the burden of conflict was to fall, a hero before whom Gibbon hushed his habitual irony and spoke as a Christian,— through all that long "warfare in the dark," Athanasius never flinched, never wavered, never repined, never despaired, never forgot that the battle was for all that men had of hope and faith.[8]

Five times Athanasius suffered exile; he faced councils and emperors; from the time when, scarcely more than a boy, he wrote the two treatises, *Contra Gentes* and *De Incarnatione,* which laid down the lines of Christian theology, from that time his pen was never long idle; while still only a deacon he was the power behind Bishop Alexander in his contentions with Arius and at Nicea, and at the age of thirty he was appointed Alexander's successor in the

[8] *Ep. ad Episc. Aeg.,* 21: Ὡς τοῦ περὶ παντὸς ὄντος ἡμῖν ἀγῶνος. With this battle-cry of the faith I like to recall the Sophoclean line, λόγων γὰρ οὐ νῦν ἐστιν ἀγών, ἀλλὰ σῆς ψυχῆς πέρι (*Electra,* 1491), and the words which may have come from the mouth of Socrates himself: μέγας ὁ ἀγών, μέγας, οὐχ ὅσος δοκεῖ, τὸ χρηστὸν ἢ κακὸν γενέσθαι. καλὸν γὰρ τὸ ἆθλον καὶ ἡ ἐλπὶς μεγάλη (*Republic* 608B, *Phaedo* 114C).

storm centre of the Church. He succeeded, as
perhaps no other man ever did, in showing a
restless and militant activity without ever losing his central calm and peace; his whole life
reads like an almost incredible romance.

The first serious move against him was a vile
conspiracy, including the charge that he had
murdered a certain Arsenius, Bishop of Hyp-
sele in the Thebaid, and had mutilated the
corpse for purposes of sorcery. His accusers
even displayed a wooden box containing a dis-
membered hand, which was all, they said, that
could be found of the missing man. By diligence, aided by curious accident, the renegade
was discovered and shamed into confession of
the plot. The next step was startlingly dramatic. Athanasius was summoned to meet a synod
at Tyre, and went, accompanied by forty-eight
of his suffragans. Various malignant accusations were repudiated by him, and then, as a
last resource, this story of Arsenius was revived,
the box with the severed hand displayed, and it
was boldly declared that the man impersonat-
ing the murdered bishop was an impostor.
"Athanasius, who was prepared even for this,
looked around with calm self-possession. 'Does
anyone here,' he asked, 'know Arsenius by

sight?' 'We *did* know him well,' cried several
voices. He turned aside, and led forward a man
closely muffled up, with head bent down. 'Raise
your head.' The figure obeyed, and showed the
features of Arsenius. 'Is not this he?' Athanasius asked; and then deliberately lifted up the
cloak, first from one hand, then, after a pause,
from the other. 'You see he has two hands;
where was the third cut off?' For the moment he
enjoyed a triumph: Arcaph (one of the witnesses) ran out of the court, but his associates
exclaimed, 'It is another case of magical illusion.' Amid the uproar that followed, the Count
Dionysius, who acted as imperial commissioner,
and had a certain sense of justice, secured the
safety of Athanasius by hurrying him away."[9]
The story, told by Athanasius himself in his
Apology, is typical, alas, of the character of
many of the councils, and of the restraining influence of the Roman courts, with their inherited sense of legal procedure, upon the tumul-
tuous Orient; and it gives some notion also of

[9] From the life of Athanasius prefixed to Bright's edition of the
Orations. The best work on the man, and one of the best on the
whole period, is still Möhler's *Athanasius der Grosse,* 2nd ed.
For English readers the chapters in Farrar's *Lives of the
Fathers* may be recommended for their eloquence and their
justness of view.

the resourcefulness and grim humour of the great champion of the faith.

From Tyre Athanasius fled, with five of his suffragans, to Constantinople, where, knowing that Constantine, now in the hands of the Arians, would willingly grant him no interview, he waylaid the Emperor as he was riding into his new capital, and convinced him of the baseness of the accusations. For the moment Athanasius was victorious; but the conspirators changed their tactics, and persuaded Constantine that the bishop had threatened to stop the ships which carried corn from Alexandria to Constantinople. This touched the Emperor on a tender spot, and Athanasius was relegated to Gaul, his first exile.

Another incident, and we must leave this interesting subject. The exile was back in Alexandria, and Constantius, the son of Constantine, an avowed friend of the Arians, was now master of the world. It is February the eighth of the year 355, and Athanasius is holding an all-night service in the Church of Saint Thomas, when the Prefect of Egypt comes with a body of armed soldiers to arrest him in the name of the Emperor. The bishop, as he tells the story in his *Apology,* was sitting on the episcopal throne and had ordered the deacon to read the 136th Psalm, while the people gave the response: "For His mercy endureth forever." This was done and the congregation was about to go home, when the soldiers broke open the doors and rushed into the sanctuary, trampling down many and forcing their way towards the chancel. Those about Athanasius called to him to escape, but he refused to do so until the people had all got away. "So I stood up," he says, "and called for prayer, and desired all to go out before me. . . . And when the greater part had gone, and the rest were following, the monks who were there, and certain of the clergy, came up and dragged me away." And so, by the Lord's guidance and help, he adds, he escaped through the throng of soldiers unobserved, praising God mightily that he had been able to save the people before his own rescue. Then, after an interval of struggle, followed the most dramatic period of exile, while he lived in the Egyptian wilderness, concealed by the faithful monks, and passed secretly from monastery to monastery as the pursuit became hot. Strange adventures befell him, and still amidst all his hardships he issued those appeals to the orthodox which made him if anything more hated by the enemy than when he was in power.

It was during this period of Athanasius' exile, the third, that for a moment all appeared to be lost. Under threats of the Emperor, the western bishops, who had met in council at Rimini and were dragged thence to the inhospitable town of Nikê in Thrace, half starved and frozen, utterly wearied out, signed at last a creed which, though ostensibly orthodox, virtually abrogated the Nicene Faith. It was of this moment that Jerome afterwards wrote his famous sentence: "The world groaned in amazement to find itself Arian." And it was for the constancy of one man while all the world yielded or despaired that the still more famous phrase went out: *Athanasius contra mundum.*

The lives of the ancient Fathers are not always pleasant reading, and particularly after the union of Church and State under Constantine there arose a species of theological politicians who combined worldly ambition with religious zeal in a manner which, to say the least, is not edifying. But of this taint there is no trace in Athanasius, and I do not know where else in history one meets a man who exhibits so complete a devotion to a contested truth

with such tenacity of will yet with never a
breath of self-seeking vanity. In Athanasius
we see the miracle performed of a saint without
egotism. His works, written mainly for immediate effect and with no thought of literary
performance, may seem on a hasty perusal to
have lost their interest along with the contro-
versies in which he was engaged. You will not
find in his occasional tracts any of those subtleties which attract the modern mind in Clement and the two Gregories, and you may at first
be inclined to attribute his limpid clarity to
shallowness of thought. But on further acquaintance one begins to realize that this simplicity of manner is not incompatible with, is
in fact significant of, the profoundest insight
into spiritual truth. It is not Origen or Augustine or any other of the Fathers, neither is it
Thomas Aquinas or any other of the scholas-
tics, who should be reckoned the great philosopher of Christianity, but Athanasius. In that
respect also he stands *contra mundum*. After
St. Paul and the writer of the fourth Gospel
he is the creator of our faith, and without him
it is not an exaggeration to say there would
have been no enduring Church. Well might
Hooker declare of him: "Only in Athanasius

there was nothing observed throughout the course of that long tragedy other than such as very well became a wise man to do and a righteous to suffer. So that this was the plain condition of those times: the whole world against Athanasius, and Athanasius against it; half a hundred of years spent in doubtful trial which of the two in the end should prevail, the side which had all, or else the part which had no friend but God and death, the one a defender of his innocency, the other a finisher of all his troubles."[10]

The third exile was, as we have seen, the time of the Council of Rimini and of the sharpest peril to the Church; but it was in these same years that two young men from Cappadocia, Basil of Neocaesarea and Gregory of Nazianzus, were studying together at the University of Athens, fitting themselves with all the learning of the schools in preparation for their life work as champions of the Nicene Faith. In their mind Athanasius was, as Gregory afterwards called him in a magnificent funeral oration, equal to some, superior to others, of the prophets, priests, apostles, evangelists, and doctors, who from Enoch to his own day were

10 *Ecclesiastical Polity*, V, xlii, 5.

the types and preachers of the incarnate
Christ.[11] On these Cappadocians, with the
other, and less prominent, Gregory of Nyssa,
the mantle of the Christian Elijah was to fall.
And to them came the victory. In 380 Gregory
Nazianzen, then Bishop of Constantinople, de-
livered his five Theological Orations, directed
against the dregs of Arianism; and at Constantinople in the next year the second ecumenical
council, summoned and sanctioned by Theodosius I, the Great, declared "that the Nicene
Faith [including the *homoousios*] must be
maintained and all heresies anathematized."
And at the same time—so the irony of fate, or
of human nature, willed—the assembly allowed, or virtually compelled, the spokesman
of that Faith to resign his episcopal seat.
Henceforth Arianism might flourish among
the barbarians of the Empire, and might in a
new form be revived at the Reformation, but
it could never again claim the position of orthodoxy. The Church was saved.

[11] *In Laudem Athanasii*, 3, 4.

CHAPTER VII

ANTIOCH AND LAODICEA

THE second ecumenical council, at Constantinople in 381, by confirming the Faith of Nicea
had settled definitely and, so far as the standard
of the Church was concerned, finally what may
be called the theological problem raised by belief in the divine Sonship. Meanwhile a new set
of heresies was springing up, similar ultimately
in their source to Sabellianism and Arianism but
directed not so much to the relation of Christ
the Word to God as to the problem of Christ's
own composite nature. The battle-ground was
thus shifted from theology to what is more
specifically Christology. Admit the full divinity of Christ as Nicea demanded. Very well.
What then is to be said of his manhood? This
Jesus, who brought a unique revelation of the
Word to men, a person to be known and loved
and adored, was yet in some way a complete
human being like ourselves. How could this be?

The various Christological heresies answered
bluntly, or diplomatically: It was not. And
each after its fashion proceeded to unfold a
theoretical explanation of the facts which
should at once avoid the dilemma in a manner
satisfactory to reason, while retaining the
Christian object of worship. And here again,
as there are two possible ways of solving the
paradox, so there were two great heretical
schools of Christology; the old gigantomachy
had to be fought over with freshly armed foes.
Stated in the baldest terms, one party, the
Nestorians, declared that, if you insist on the
two distinct natures of Christ, then you must
admit also two persons somehow acting together; whereas another party, the Monophysites (from *monos,* "one," and *physis,* "nature"), avowed that, if you cling to Christ as a
single person to be worshipped, then you must
also reduce the apparent double nature to one
by absorbing his manhood in his Godhead. To
both of which sects the Church responded with
a blank *caveat.* That is the history, in a nut-
shell so to speak, of the second great contention between heresy and orthodoxy. But there
were preliminary skirmishes before the main
battle was engaged.

Now to hold a clue to the intricacies of this history, in which friend and foe were often intermingled in a manner which only embittered while it embroiled the conflict, we must for a while look at the changing fortune of certain words as they passed from party to party and as their use was finally determined by common consent. We have seen that the sting of the Nicene Faith lay in the term *homoousios*. And in that document *ousia* and *hypostasis* (as essence or substance) are used indifferently, so that, translating the language of the early divines, we can say with equal correctness that the Son was "coessential" or "consubstantial" with the Father. *Ousia* and *hypostasis* were borrowed from the language of philosophy, not from Scripture (hence in part the hostility to them), and signified the central reality of a thing, its innermost being; they were more technical names for its *physis,* its genuine final "nature." These three words, then—essence and substance and nature—were virtually synonymous among the earliest theologians, and were sufficient so long as the debate turned on the essential, or substantial, or natural, kinship of Christ with God. Even Athanasius felt no need to differentiate amongst them.

But with the subsequent question of Christology it became necessary to invent terms which should maintain a certain distinction between Christ and God while not breaking the unity of the Godhead, and should also express a distinction between the Godhead and the manhood of Christ while not reducing the Incarnation to a mechanical partnership of a God and a man. The problem was not easy, it must be confessed, nor was it quickly solved. In reaching an answer the terms *ousia* and *physis* were left intact and synonymous, as signifying the ultimate "essence" or "nature," whether it be that which Christ possesses in common with God or that which he possesses in common with man. But *hypostasis* gradually underwent a change, made possible by the peculiar flexibility of the Greek language. Originally the compound by the preposition *hypo* indicated that which stood *under* an external appearance as the essential nature of a thing; now, with the fresh turn of the debate, it assumed a new force and began to signify, still an ultimate reality, but the individual reality which stood *under,* so to speak, a general reality, and so could be applied to the Godhead of the Father and the Godhead of the Son as two substances

or, as the word might now be more exactly
translated, two "subsistences" (*hypostaseis*),
while by their common essence there was but
one God.[1] We can follow the introduction and
development of this verbal discrimination quite
clearly in the polemical works of the Cappadocians, but I think the reader will gladly be
spared the proof by illustrations. The matter
is summed up sufficiently well in the saying of
Basil: "Since then in our contemplation we
must speak of something common in the Holy
Trinity and of something individual, that
which we speak of as common we refer to the
ousia [he might also have said *physis*], while
the *hypostasis* is the individual mark of each."[2]

Further, since this distinction of individuals
was introduced into the monotheism inherited
from the Jews by no ontological considerations
but by the concrete fact that a new revelation

[1] Hence the Greek formula for the Trinity, μία οὐσία ἐν τρισὶν
ὑποστάσεσιν, preferable in my judgement to the language of
Tertullian. It is to be noted that the *hypostasis* of theology becomes something different from the *hypostasis* of metaphysics
as *e.g.* in Plotinus: Ὑπόστασιν δὲ εἶναι καὶ οὐσίαν ἐξ οὐσίας ἐλάττω
μὲν τῆς ποιησαμένης, οὖσαν δὲ ὅμως, ἀπιστεῖν οὐ προσήκει. This definition
might serve the purpose of Arius, but in the orthodox view an
hypostasis is not an *ousia* lower than another *ousia*, but an in-
dividualization within an *ousia*.

[2] *Epist.* xxxviii, 5: Ἐπεὶ οὖν τὸ μέν τι κοινὸν ἐν τῇ ἁγίᾳ Τριάδι τὸ δὲ
ἰδιάζον ὁ λόγος ἐνεθεώρησεν, ὁ μὲν τῆς κοινότητος λόγος εἰς τὴν οὐσίαν
ἀνάγεται, ἡ δὲ ὑπόστασις τὸ ἰδιάζον ἑκάστου σημεῖόν ἐστιν. —
Cf. *Epist.* ccxxxvi (Migne 884A).

of God had come through the life and character of Jesus Christ, it is natural that the word *hypostasis,* as soon as it was differentiated from *ousia,* should come to signify "a particular centre of conscious being,"[3] and so should coalesce with *prosôpon,* the nearest expression in Greek to our word "person." Hence the final equation of *ousia* (being) with *physis* (nature), and of *hypostasis* (subsistence) with *prosôpon* (person).[4]

But it is important to remember also that these words retained always something of the fluidity which characterizes Greek thought. Thus, though "person" is the best translation we have for *prosôpon,* the Greek word never acquired in ancient terminology quite the sharp definition of our English equivalent. "It is always," as Professor Bethune-Baker observes, "a person looked at from some distinctive point of view, a person in particular cir-

---

[3] Srawley, note on Gregory Nyssen, *Cat. Or.,* i.
[4] *Prosôpon* means literally "the face," and more especially the face as expressive of a mood or temper, as in the phrase of Sophocles (*Oed. Tyr.,* 532): ἢ τοσόνδ' ἔχεις τόλμης πρόσωπον, "Hast thou a face (or, front) so bold?" In this way the word may be used as a virtual equivalent for the mask, προσωπεῖον, which denotes the particular character of an actor as he appears on the stage; and so from the meaning of a "person represented" the transition is easy to the simpler meaning of "person" itself, or "personality." (Cf. Epictetus, I, xxix, 43, 45, and the title of I, i.)

cumstances; that is, it conveys the notion much
more of the environment than of the subject.
It expresses in its ecclesiastical usage in a
single word precisely what Basil's *tropos hy-
parxeôs* (manner of existence) denoted, and
what *hypostasis* was ultimately narrowed down
to mean."[5] The Greek terminology for the
Trinity, or more particularly for the relation
of the first two members of the Trinity, avoids
the metaphysical difficulties forced upon us by
the very clarity of our modern vocabulary.
There may be a virtue in vagueness when we
undertake to give names to the undefinable. It
is not quite the same thing to speak of two
hypostaseis, or *prosôpa,* having the same *ousia,*
as to say there are two "persons" in one God.

All this may sound rather like the pedantry
of philology than like the life of religion, but in
fact it is impossible to follow the debates of the

---

[5] *Introduction to the Early History of Christian Doctrine,* 234.
Professor Bethune-Baker is here referring to the Latin word
persona, but the comment applies equally well to πρόσωπον,
which in fact was imported into Greek theology as a translation
of the Latin term. Tertullian, finding no equivalent in Latin for
the distinction between οὐσία and ὑπόστασις had translated the
former by *substantia* and the latter by *persona.* Then by reflex
influence *persona* was turned into πρότωπον, as a synonym of
ὑπόστασις. In one respect πρόσωπον, whatever other difficulties
may have clung to it, had this advantage, that it is free of the
legal associations which belong to *persona,* and which helped to
strengthen the legalistic tone of Western theology.

fourth and fifth centuries without understanding the elusive nature of the terms the contestants were obliged to use, corresponding to the no less elusive character of the doctrines they were attempting to express. And as the question of heresy must be constantly raised in our discussion of these men, it is desirable to set down here, though chronologically out of place, the so-called Definition of Chalcedon, in which the fourth ecumenical council (in 451) established once for all the orthodox use of the four words involved:

"Wherefore, after the example of the Holy Fathers, we all with one voice confess our Lord Jesus Christ one and the same Son, the same perfect in Godhead, the same perfect in manhood, very God and very man, the same consisting of a reasonable soul and a body, of one substance (*homoousios*) with the Father as touching the Godhead, the same of one substance with us as touching the manhood, like us in all things, sin except; begotten of the Father before the worlds as touching the Godhead, the same in these last days, for us and for our salvation, born of the Virgin Mary, the Mother of God (*Theotokos*), as touching the manhood, one and the same Christ, Son, Lord, Only-begotten, to be acknowledged of two natures (*physeis*), without confusion, without conversion, without

division, never to be separated; the distinction
of natures being in no wise done away because
of the union, but rather the characteristic property of each nature being preserved, and con-
curring into one Person (*prosôpon*) and one
subsistence (*hypostasis*), not as if Christ were
parted or divided into two Persons, but one and
the same Son and Only-begotten God, Word,
Lord, Jesus Christ; even as the Prophets from
the beginning spake concerning Him, and our
Lord Jesus Christ hath instructed us, and the
Symbol of the Fathers hath handed down to
us."

I suspect that the first effect of this document on a mind not inured to the methods of
theological dispute will be a feeling of repulsion for its pedantic tautology; but I think also
that a second reading and a little reflection will
somewhat modify this attitude. It will appear
that, however crabbed the language may sound,
the purpose of the document is simply this, and
nothing more: to restate the *homoousios* of the
Nicene Faith as the basis of theology, and to
assert, emphatically and uncompromisingly,
the inevitable corollary, that as Christ in his
eternal Godhead is of the same nature (or essence, or substance) as the Father, so after the
Incarnation he remains one person, or subsist-

ence, but now with a double nature. Later we
shall have occasion to discuss the philosophical
implications of the Niceo-Chalcedonian dogma.
Here it will not be out of place to call attention to this very significant fact, that, while the
usage of the four Christological terms so long
bandied about is now settled once for all, there
is no attempt to define their meaning. The "essence," or "nature," is left merely as a name
for that wherein we think of Christ as divine
and for that wherein we think of him as human,
the "subsistence" or "person" is merely a name
for the seat of unity within himself. And it is
equally significant—though the fact has been
too often overlooked by the historians of dogma—that this deliberate refraining of the desire to go behind what we must accept or reject
as ultimate facts stands out as a singular event
in the annals of theology, as the shadow, I
would say, of a great rock in a thirsty land.
Before Chalcedon it was the heretics who in
one way or another made mischief by their endeavour to define the mystery of the divine
economy in terms satisfactory to reason; after
Chalcedon it was, unfortunately, the Church
herself in her councils who yielded to the seduc-
tion of rationalism and thus barely escaped, if

so be she did escape, the pitfalls of error. It is not within the scope of this work to follow the later course of theology, but a word or two must be said here about the fifth and sixth general councils, to illustrate what I mean by this deflection of orthodoxy into the dubious paths already trod by the feet of condemned heretics.

The change from the dogmatic spirit which prevailed in the fourth council to the metaphysical spirit which dominated the two successive councils may be described in a few sentences taken from Harnack, who in this matter shows a soundness of historical judgement not always found in his works. "In the course of the transition from the fifth to the sixth century Aristotelianism once more became the fashion in science." The man who introduced this method into theology was Leontius of Byzantium (c. 485-543), "the first scholastic. . . . He treated of substance, genus, species, individual being, of the attributes which constitute the substance, of inseparable accidents and of separable accidents. It was on the result of these discussions that the conceptions of the natures and the *hypostasis* in Christ were based. . . . In the whole way in which Leontius transferred the Nesto-

rian-Monophysite controversy into the region
of philosophy [*i.e.* metaphysics], we may accordingly see a momentous revolution. . . .
The Chalcedonian dogma is lost in philosophical [*i.e.* metaphysical] theology. Here, too, for
this reason, the work for the historian of dogma
ceases: his place is taken by the historian of
theology."[6]

This was a revolution, I should add, which
through the Neoplatonism of Augustine af-
fected the West as well as the East, and the
consequences of which are more far-reaching
than is commonly recognized. It marks the
moment when the Greek tradition, developing
the doctrine of Plato, came to an end and scholasticism began; it explains how the later councils, for our purpose the fifth and sixth, though
they did not repudiate the Definition of Chalcedon, but ostensibly confirmed it, and though
they bristled with anathemas against innumerable heretics, really committed the Church to a

6 *History of Dogma*, IV, 232-234. Cf. the statement of Loofs
quoted by Harnack: "The philosophical theory upon which the
arguments of our author (Leontius) rests has a decidedly
Aristotelian and not a Platonic origin." After the ridicule cast
on Bishop Hampden by Mozley and the other Tractarians of
Oxford and the doubts raised as to the integrity of his learning,
it may be temerarious to take his *Bampton Lectures* seriously;
but really I know of no book which shows a clearer insight into
the mischief done to religion by the fundamental rationalism
of the scholastic philosophy.

theological method implicitly heretical. The point is this: the fourth council simply stated categorically a dogma concerning the personality and natures of Christ in such a manner as to lift it out of the field of tortuous discussion; the fifth and sixth councils, not content with this bare statement of what was held to be a superrational truth, undertook, like the condemned heresies, and in precisely their method, to define the terms of this truth.

Thus the fifth council, held at Constantinople in 553 under Justinian, seeing the difficulties for reason in the Chalcedonian formula, "of (or, in) two natures," proceeded to explain *how* there could be two natures in one person, with the conclusion that "the difference between them is to be understood only theoretically, . . . since there is one from both." In other words it adopted the docetism of its master, Justinian, and by leaving only a theoretical humanity in Christ virtually fell into the trap of Monophysitism.

Then came a revulsion which brought the contrary error of Nestorianism to the surface. In the seventh century the theologians of the East became concerned with the thorny psychological question whether there was one will or two wills in Christ; that is to say: did he possess one will identified with his personality, or two wills identified respectively with his two natures? If you accept the former hypothesis, then his lower nature is left without a will and his humanity seems to remain incomplete as in the heresy of Apollinarius. If on the other hand you accept the second hypothesis, then you seem to introduce two persons, since the will as the highest and most central faculty of man is scarcely distinguishable from what we mean by personality. The sixth council, held in 680 again at Constantinople, declared for the two wills, anathematizing those who adhered to the theory of one will as Monophysites, and thus, by its so-called doctrine of Dyotheletism, committed the Church to a form of Christology virtually condemned in Nestorius.[7] The bishops, before falling into this snare for the overwise, should have remembered the ancient maxims, Do not stir up Camarina, and Do not move what should be left undisturbed.

Now, with the Definition of Chalcedon in our hands as a touchstone, and with the two ensuing councils as a warning, we may return

[7] See T. A. Lacey in the *Guardian* of December 23, 1921.

to the labyrinth of Christological disputes. The trouble began at Antioch, where at an earlier date Paul of Samosata and Lucian had sown the seeds of Arianism, and where there had always been a tendency to emphasize the human side against the inclination of Alexandria to throw into relief the divine side of Christ's life; just as in their exegesis the scholars of Antioch clung to the more literal meaning of Scripture in opposition to the allegorizing method introduced by Philo and Origen. From this centre the new movement, spreading out, came to a head under Diodore of Tarsus and his pupil, Theodore of Mopsuestia, whose doctrine was formulated as a protest against the teaching of Apollinarius. Theodore, in particular, was a man of irreproachable character and one of the most noted of biblical commentators. He died in 428, and only a hundred years later, at a time when theology was perhaps at its lowest ebb, fell under condemnation as a heretic.

It is not easy to form a clear notion of the Antiochian Christology as it was developed by these sectaries. In their zeal to maintain the complete humanity of the incarnate Word they seem to have identified the nature (*physis*) and person (*prosôpon*) of Christ, which were to be, and by the great Cappadocians already had been, carefully distinguished; but how far this was merely a verbal confusion and how far it signified a real departure from the orthodox view, we hesitate to say. Theodore at one time avows succinctly that in Christ the manhood as well as the Godhead was perfect in nature and *person,* which can only mean, taken literally, that two persons existed together in Jesus as well as two natures. He even declares, quite categorically, that there were two Sons, one born of God, the other of David, each complete and separate; yet elsewhere he as categorically asserts that the two natures make by their union one person, and repudiates the doctrine of two Sons as a slander. From this laxity of language one can see how the Council of Chalcedon was driven to every device of statement to set these shifting terms in their right place once for all.

Perhaps we come closer to Theodore's point of view when we turn from the word "union" to his more favourite expression "indwelling" (*enoikêsis*). By this he means that the Godhead dwells in the complete man Jesus, not by His essence or energy, which would imply a return to the discarded heresy of Sabellius and the monarchians, but by His "good-will" or "pleasure" (*eudokia*). This last word, which is characteristic of the Antiochian school, was brought into the debate from St. Paul's usage in Ephesians, where (i, 5) he speaks of our adoption through Jesus Christ "according to the *good pleasure* of his will," and again (i, 9) of "the mystery of his will, according to his *good pleasure*," whereby he hath proposed in the fulness of times to resume and renew all things in Christ. *Eudokia* is thus scarcely more than a paraphrase for God's eternal will or purpose to redeem mankind,[8] and was chosen, we suspect, because it seems by its vagueness to avoid the troublesome questions raised by too close an inspection of the Incarnation. In all men, Theodore would appear to say, God dwells in so far as by the excellence of their disposition they meet with His good pleasure; but in Jesus there was an indwelling so different in degree as to be different in kind from the inspiration of the prophets, so full and complete that the man thus chosen was raised to

---

[8] It is thus used by Athanasius, *Contra Ar.*, iii, 63: Τὰ μὲν γένητα εὐδοκίᾳ καὶ βουλήσει γέγονεν, ὁ δὲ υἱὸς οὐ θελήματός ἐστι δημιούργημα ἐπιγεγονώς. Rather the Logos is the ζῶσα βουλή of God, the θέλημα τοῦ Πατρός, and Athanasius might almost have said ἡ εὐδοκία τοῦ θεοῦ.

partake of the honour belonging to the Son
who dwells in God by nature. The union thus
becomes a junction of wills so close as to produce the effect, if not the literal actuality, of
one person—the good will of God condescending to man, the moral will of a man conforming
itself to God. As Swete expresses the matter:
"In Jesus He dwells, according to Scripture,
'as in a Son': and this means that, while between the human and divine nature in Jesus
there is complete distinctness, yet there is also
such a unity of will and of operation that the
result is one Person."[9]

I fear this will not be very lucid to the
reader; it certainly is not lucid to me, as I
suspect it was not to Theodore himself. The
curious point is that these Antiochenes were
avowed Aristotelians, who in the name of reason accused their antagonists of confusing the
simple issue of religion—*tantam confusionem
rationi pietatis introducentes.* By their theory
of *eudokia* they apparently had in mind to
avoid the Platonic realism which would hypos-
tatize the Logos of God as a living individual
entity, and to bring the scheme of the Incarnation into the field of rational psychology.

9 *Theod. Mops. on Minor Epistles of S. Paul,* II, 295 f.

Their aim was plausible, but in fact they only succeeded in escaping paradox by falling into confusion;—there are not wanting theologians today who are more comfortable when concealed in the dusk of pseudo-science than when faced with what Athanasius calls the "thing truly paradoxical."[10] A vivid light is thrown on the post-Chalcedonian deflection of the Church itself into the byways of metaphysical psychology when we consider that the fifth general council anathematized Theodore as a heretic, whereas in the next general council, with the acceptance of Dyotheletism, his error was virtually raised into a canon of orthodoxy.

The strength of these later Antiochenes, as of Paul of Samosata before them, lay in their insistence on the full manhood of Christ, without which, as the Church also held, there could be no practical scheme of salvation; their fault arose from a failure to maintain with equal insistence the perfect unity of the Saviour as a person. In the very nature of things, as the human mind is constituted, we should expect to see them opposed by a school which employed the same sort of psychology to emphasize the unity of Christ's personality by exalting

[10] *Contra Ar.*, iii, 57: Πρᾶγμα παράδοξον ἀληθῶς.

his Godhead at the expense of his manhood;
and this is what actually happened with Apollinarius of Laodicea. Here again we have to
deal with a man of stainless reputation, a
scholar of repute, a trained logician. Among
his other accomplishments was that of versifi-
cation, and when the apostate Julian struck a
blow at the Church by forbidding Christians to
teach or study the pagan authors, Apollinarius
and his father, with more diligence doubtless
than inspiration, undertook to supply the peda-
gogical place of the classics by turning out a
whole literature of biblical epics and dramas
and dialogues. Time, which robs us of so much
that is desirable, has compensated a little for
its thefts by scattering the dust of poppies on
these excogitations of the Homer and Sophocles of Laodicea. With equal hand Time, or,
more literally, the jealous hand of orthodoxy,
has buried in the same oblivion the theological
works of the school, to the grief and indignation of some who burn with the zeal of justice.
For my part I sustain the loss with equanim-
ity; I should know more of ancient theology if
I had to read less of it, and I suspect that these
suppressed heretics would lose some of their at-

traction for modern scholarship if they did not offer so magnificent a field for conjecture.

Apollinarius († 392) was a stalwart champion of Nicea against the Arians, fighting loyally for the immutability and essential sinlessness of the incarnate Logos. But in his defence of orthodoxy on this side he took a course which offended the school then represented by Diodore. The result was a merry war between Antioch and Laodicea, in which the mutual animosity was evident enough, though it is not quite so plain which was the aggressor and which the defendant. Meanwhile the poor Church, stumbling along in the middle of the way, received the fire from both sides, and groaned.

The point from which Apollinarius made his attack is clear, and his method can be defined almost in a sentence. His answer to the Antiochenes, whom he classes always with the followers of Paul of Samosata, proceeds from a plausible psychology, which, by a system of trichotomy derived apparently from Jewish and Greek sources, divides human nature into reason, soul, and flesh. These are the constituent factors of our common manhood; but in the Apollinarian scheme—and here the trouble

began—not of Christ's. Now in the thought of
the age generally that which gives to man his
individual character and self-consciousness,
that which may be called his personality, was
the reason, or logos. And so, by his tripartite
division of man, Apollinarius saw a device to
save the union in Christ of the two natures,
human and divine, and at the same time to
avoid the absurdity of admitting two persons in
Jesus, as the Antiochenes were virtually forced
to do. He would simply decapitate, so to speak,
the human nature of Christ, leaving it to consist of flesh and soul without reason, and so
without the disturbing factor of personality.
This missing element should be supplied by the
Son of God, who, as the Logos, is pure reason
and perfect personality. And there you are: the
Incarnation presents you with a single person
having its own nature, which then takes to itself
the lower nature of man without human personality. In Christ there are thus two natures, as
orthodoxy demands, but so combined as to
leave no place for sin or temptation, since these
are the errors of human reason, as the guiding
principle, and there is no human reason in
Christ to err. He is a composite being precisely
as are you and I, save that his highest and

dominant faculty comes from heaven and is consubstantial with God. The blasphemy of the Arians is averted, the impossible psychology of the Antiochenes is circumvented, the rationalism of the schools can find no flaw in so cleverly devised a dualism, the faith of Christianity is justified. "Oh new creation and marvellous mingling," Apollinarius exclaimed of his own invention. Yet withal the Church, infatuated with its love of paradox and unreason, repudiated the Laodicean Christology as it did that of Antioch. Apollinarianism was condemned at Alexandria in 362; it was attacked by the Cappadocians; condemned again in synods at Rome and Antioch; flatly pronounced to be heresy at the second general council in 381, and left as such by the two succeeding councils. It remains heresy; yet it was all but sanctioned by the fifth council, when the flood of metaphysical psychology swept through the barriers of Chalcedon into the Church.

In the attitude of the orthodox theologians towards Apollinarius there are various phases to be noted. At the beginning of his career, as an avowed advocate of Nicea and as a stalwart opponent of the clearly heretical Arians, not to

mention the Sabellians and the dubious Antiochenes, he quite naturally had the support of
the Church. And in particular Athanasius,
whose whole life was spent in conflict with the
Arians, and who had received personal assist-
ance from Apollinarius, was willing to overlook any minor deviations of his friend; he was
in fact conciliatory by temperament, except
where the divinity of Christ came into play.
And so too with the Cappadocian leaders, fric-
tion only came when it appeared that the
Laodicean, in his antagonism to the over-em-
phasis of Christ's manhood at Antioch, had
fallen into the contrary extreme. Even then the
gage of hostility was at first taken up with reluctance and in self-defense; the aggression
was from the other side. We can see in the correspondence of Gregory Nazianzen how he was
dragged into the conflict only after his home
town had been stirred up into faction by the
active propaganda of the Apollinarians, and
how difficult he found it to formulate a reply
to the clever logic of the enemy. Even that
heresy-hunter of ill repute among all modern
scholars, the fanatical Epiphanius of Salamis,
laments the necessity of exposing the errors of
one whom personally he admires. "Why," he

exclaims, "do persons of the kind play the busybody with God, fabricating their shameful speculations about matters that no prophet nor evangelist nor apostle nor writer has thought necessary to discuss? . . . Infinite harm, in the creation of hatred and faction. For when once discussion arises it produces panic."[11]

But, the gauntlet once taken up, the method of attack was clear. The whole meaning of the Incarnation lay in the fact that the Logos of God had been born as man, had so united himself with human nature as to redeem it from the consequences of the Fall. This was implied in the very motto of Christology formulated by Irenaeus and established by Athanasius: "God became man in order that man might become God." How then shall we understand this act of redemption, where shall we look for real salvation, if the Son of God did not in truth become the Son of man, but merely assumed inanimate flesh, or flesh and soul, without that faculty which distinguishes man from the brutes and makes him really human, and which also, as the real seat of sin, is the part that needs to be renovated and redeemed? So the champions of the traditional faith de-

11 *Adv. Haer.*, lxxvii, 18.

manded in many tones, and to their inquiry no
satisfactory answer could be returned.

In one respect the antagonism of the Church
to Apollinarius has been subjected to harsh
criticism on the part of modern scholars. Did
he, or did he not, carry the union of the Logos
to such a degree of intimacy as to teach that the
flesh of the Lord was itself also of celestial
origin and no true human body at all? Did he
eliminate even this poor relic of humanity except in name? There can be no doubt of the fact
that this was the onus of the charges laid against
him by his contemporary judges, and the only
question is whether they were attacking a man
of straw or the real Apollinarius. To certain
critics of today it seems clear that his doctrine
in this respect was either woefully misunderstood or wilfully misrepresented; they argue
that belief in a celestial descent of the flesh was
quite inconsistent with the Apollinarian psychology. The inconsistency may be admitted;
but the question remains: who was inconsistent,
the convicted heretic or his nominally orthodox
accusers? The "liberal" historian of today almost instinctively replies: The orthodox accusers, of course. To me the answer is not so
simple. In the first place it must be remembered

that the Apollinarian heresy was no hole-and-corner affair, but conducted an aggressive propaganda over a large part of the eastern world. I hold it incredible that men like Basil and the two Gregories, to name no others, should have been far astray in their interpretation of the doctrine, or should have foisted upon it so wild a fancy, with no justification.[12]

The desire to rehabilitate a man of Apollinarius' character may be both charitable and honourable; but an irritating note is introduced with the assertion that if Apollinarius is condemned for heresy, then Athanasius, the accepted champion of orthodoxy, must be condemned with him. Now it is true that in his bitter life-and-death struggle with the Arians Athanasius was led to dwell much on the Godhead and comparatively less on the manhood of Christ; but that is a very different thing from saying that his view of the Incarnation was in any proper sense of the word Apollinarian. Some of the turns of modern criticism are hard to understand. I confess that for myself difficulty of understanding passes into bewilderment when I hear that the biblical scholarship of Apollinarius did not "allow him to follow

12 See Appendix C.

Athanasius and expurgate from the Gospels the mark of the Lord's humanity."[13] Certainly, if there be any fault in the Christology of Athanasius, it is not that he expurgates the manhood of Christ, but that he sets the manhood side by side with the Godhead in too harsh, in what might almost be called too mechanical, a dualism. It is true, of course, that to designate the humanity of the Incarnate he follows the fourth Gospel and the Greek Fathers generally in using the term "flesh" (*sarx*) ; but he is careful to state repeatedly that by "flesh" he means "man,"[14] and in page after page of his works, in virtually the whole of his third *Oration Against the Arians,* he makes it plain that with the "flesh" he includes the "soul" (*psyché*), meaning thereby the spirit and mind and thought and reason as well as the sensual desires. "Flesh" is a proper word for man, because the human soul, and primarily the reason, or logos, has fallen from its high vocation to a degraded subservience to the body.[15] Athanasius could be a friend of Apollinarius, as of Marcellus or of any one who stood with him

[13] Charles E. Raven, *Apollinarianism,* 202.
[14] *E.g. De Synodis,* 28.
[15] This will appear clearly when in a later chapter we come to study the Athanasian conception of evil.

against the most dangerous enemy of the faith, but the psychological subtleties of the Laodicean probably puzzled him as they puzzle the reader today, while the truncation of Christ's humanity he would have rejected utterly. The disciples of Apollinarius were in no doubt about the relation of Athanasius to their master in the matter of dogma. Thus Polemon places Athanasius with the Cappadocians as belonging rather to the school of Antioch than to that of Laodicea; and Eunomius holds the same view.[16]

This effort to reinstate Apollinarius, or to implicate Athanasius with him in heresy, is unfortunately not an isolated case, but belongs to a widespread movement among German scholars, and those of England who trail after them. We see the same tendency in the curious eulogy of the maddest of the Gnostics at the expense of the Christian Apologists; in the praise of Origen to the derogation of Athanasius; in the endeavour to make Paul of Samosata an orthodox and misunderstood theologian; in the contention that Nestorianism or Monophysitism (either you will, if only it be a supposed heresy) is the true interpretation of the creed; that, wherever you turn, "the heretic was less

---

[16] Lietzmann, *Apollinaris von Laodicea*, 276.

in error than the saint." Some excuse may be
found for this odd perversion of the historical
sense among scholars who are writing at a time
when if one will be famous—or will advance
his position—one must be original. That necessity is peculiarly strong in the close competition
of modern academic life. But the real source of
the evil lies, I think, even deeper than that. One
cannot go far in the literature of the so-called
liberal Protestant theology without discovering a latent, sometimes an openly avowed, an-
tipathy to everything savouring of the classical
orthodoxy; at any hazard, at any cost, it must
be proved that the traditional judgements are
wrong, that what the world has accounted
heretical is really orthodox, or *vice versa,* and
that the true understanding of things spiritual
began with the Reformation as a special privilege of the Teutonic mind. I may seem to be
exaggerating, but I am not; enlightenment has
come to me painfully, slowly; forced upon me
by the laborious re-reading of many texts to
check this or that current theory. The virtue of
the Germans is their diligence, and we cannot
dispense with them; but they have covered the
history of religion with vast clouds of dust.
With the Roman bias on one side and the con-

ceit of "liberal theology" on the other, the poor
lover of truth is hard put to it. But at least one
always knows where the Roman stands and
what his point of view will be; one can make
the proper allowances. As between the two, the
Roman historians of dogma are in the main less
misleading than the liberal Protestant.

CHAPTER VIII

THE CLIMAX OF HERESY

APOLLINARIANISM was formerly rejected at a general council, the second, in 381; the rival theology did not suffer this fate until fifty years later, and then in its Nestorian form, at the third council in Ephesus. We first know of Nestorius as abbot of a monastery near Antioch, and as a distinguished preacher and exegete of the school of Diodore and Theodore. In 428 he was called to Constantinople as patriarch of that metropolis. In his consecration sermon he is said to have addressed the Emperor, Theodosius II, in these ominous words: "Give me the earth purged of heretics, and I will give you heaven in return; help me to harry the heretics, and I will help you to harry the Persians."[1] For a season it went well with Nestorius, and ill with the Arians, Novatians, and other schismatics; but after no long while

[1] Socrates, *Hist. Ec.,* vii, 29.

he himself fell under the suspicion of another
heresy-hunter of a different stamp, Cyril of
Alexandria, and the tables were turned with a
vengeance. The very heavens were rent with the
clamours and counter-clamours of the contestants, until in 431 Cyril, by despotic manipula-
tion of a council convened before the delegates
favourable to his enemy had arrived, succeeded
in having what he called Nestorianism anathematized, and in having Nestorius deposed and
excommunicated. Later by the use of bribery at
court he drove the broken man into exile, where
he languished until just before or after the
Council of Chalcedon. There is a note of tragic
irony in the words written by Nestorius in his
decline: "I, who had been long-suffering unto
heretics, was harassed by thee so as to be driven
out; and thou wast bishop of Alexandria and
thou didst get hold of the church of Constantinople—a thing which the bishop of no other
city whatsoever would have suffered."[2] There

2 From *The Bazaar of Heracleides*, p. 96, written by Nestorius
in exile as an apology for his life. This document was discovered
in a Syriac translation in 1897, and was published in a French
version by F. Nau in 1910. An English translation with comment
was published by G. R. Driver and L. Hodgson in 1925. But
full use of the document had already been made by J. F.
Bethune-Baker in his *Nestorius and His Teaching* and by
Loofs in his *Nestorius and His Place in the History of Christian
Doctrine*. The *Bazaar* is an extraordinary book, a treasure-

may be doubts as to the relative orthodoxy of
the views held by the Lords of Constantinople
and of Alexandria; no impartial student of
history will deny that the politics of Cyril were
high-handed.

I, and the reader with me, may be relieved of
the task of analysing the doctrine of Nestorius
in detail, since it is little more than a continuation of what he had learnt from his master at
Antioch; but something must be said of a word
of ominous import, *Theotokos,* "Mother of
God,"[3] about which the storm was now raging,
as formerly it raged about the *homoousios.*
How Apollinarius had understood the term
may be seen from his own language: "If the
Word became flesh, then, worshipping the
Word, one worships the flesh, and, worshipping
the flesh, one worships the Godhead, and the
Apostles who worshipped the body were worshipping God the Word. . . . And the Virgin
who bore the flesh from the beginning bore also

house of all the Christological heresies of the age, which Nestorius criticises often with great acumen. But the final impression, to me at least, is that the author's mind was lost in
a haze of cobweb subtleties.

[3] The Latin and English paraphrases, *Mater Dei* and Mother of
God, have a certain harshness and rigidity not felt in the Greek
compound; but the word is, to say the least, unfortunate, and
marks the progress of pagan superstition into the faith. See
Bethune-Baker, *Nestorius,* 59.

the Word, and was Mother of God (Theotokos)." Now to the Antiochenes in general, and
to Nestorius in particular, this use of the word
seemed unscriptural (as it most undoubtedly
is) and blasphemous (as it still sounds to all
Protestants and to most Anglicans). Theodore
the Antiochene bishop of Mopsuestia, had already protested that it was "madness to say
that God is born of the Virgin, . . . not God,
but the temple in which God dwelt, is born of
Mary";[4] and in the first year of his charge at
Constantinople Nestorius had denounced the
doctrine in the same terms. No harm would
have resulted, had the criticized word been the
exclusive property of the suspected Apollinarians; but unfortunately it was much in favour
with Cyril, and the occasion of Nestorius' sermon was gladly seized by him to renew the feud
between Alexandria and its upstart rival on the
Bosphorus, which had already blazed out in the
persecution of Chrysostom (also an Antiochene, though orthodox) by Cyril's uncle and
predecessor Theophilus. The poor preacher of
Constantinople, who would have yielded much
for the sake of peace, under the thumbscrew
torture of dialectic, defined and refined and

[4] Bethune-Baker, *Op. Cit.*, 58.

explained; he would accept the contested term, but with such reservations that it became an equivalent for "mother of man" or, at best, "mother of Christ."[5] In vain: Cyril was no man to dally with reservations or compromise when he had his enemy at a disadvantage.

It will be seen that Theotokos could easily be used as a shibboleth to determine a man's attitude towards the vexed question of the unity or division of the two natures in Christ. To the Laodiceans it was acceptable because they thought of the two natures as so united, that she who bore the flesh must be revered also as mother of the Godhead, and Cyril in this respect stood with them; whereas to the Antiochenes, who insisted on the completeness and separateness of each nature, it seemed that the motherhood of Mary ought to be limited sharply and expressly to the human member in the compound. The great cry of Cyril—in this anticipated by the Cappadocians and all the enemies of Antioch, whether orthodox or heretical —was that by rejecting the Theotokos Nestorius so emphasized the two natures that he left no central unity for worship, but was obliged to partition his adoration between two distinct

[5] Ἀνθρωποτόκος, Χριστοτόκος.

persons, a Son of God and a Son of man,—an
attitude both absurd and impious. Against
such a charge Nestorius protested that it was
unfair and misrepresented his views. True the
human nature assumed by our Lord in the Incarnation was complete and intact to the extent
of including that last centre of individuality,
the person; nevertheless our worship is directed
to one Son, or person, only. In his *Heracleides*
he explains his position thus:

"So God became incarnate in a man in His
own person (*prosôpon*). And He made his
(the man's) person His own person. And there
is no condescension comparable to this, that his
(the man's) person should become His own
person, and that He should give him His person. Wherefore He employed his person in that
He took it to Himself."[6]

6 I quote the translation from Bethune-Baker, p. 131. The passage will be found on p. 69 of the edition of Driver and Hodgson. In an appendix to this latter work Mr. Hodgson has an
excellent account of the history of the word *prosôpon*. He holds
that in the Nestorian usage it means not so much "person," in
our modern sense, as "appearance," and that the union is
through the overlapping or identity of the appearances of the
two natures. "At first sight," he adds, "this certainly does not
look like any real union at all. Two things which look alike are
not one thing. But such a criticism entirely misunderstands Nestorius' thought. For him the πρόσωπον is no *mere* appearance. It
is a real element in the being of a thing, without which, or if it
were other than it is, the thing would not be what it is." This is
subtle, and I think makes a shrewd guess at what Nestorius was
often trying to say in his rambling metaphysics. But in certain
passages, Nestorius virtually identifies *prosôpon* with the will,

This to Cyril was blasphemy. Like a good
Greek he was suspicious of the Nestorian word
for person, *prosôpon,* with its legal associations
from the Latin *persona* and its ambiguities
from Sabellius, and clung rather to the term
hypostasis, which was at once more colourless
and less entangled in human significations.
Thus against the Nestorian "prosôpic union,"
Cyril contended for what he called the "hypostatic union,"[7] meaning thereby that there was
no unification of two persons *post factum,* so
to speak, but that Christ was one by virtue of
his eternal divine *hypostasis,* which distinguished him as God from the *hypostasis* of the
Father, and which had no counterpart in his
humanity. The human nature of Christ was indeed complete, but it was not an *hypostasis* in

and so, if not absolutely with personality as we understand (or
pretend to understand) the word, yet with something practically
the same as personality. In effect the hypostatic union of Cyril
means that Christ has only one person, or *hypostasis,* and that
divine, while the human nature is left impersonal; the prosôpic
union of Nestorius means that two persons, *prosôpa,* are somehow merged into the appearance of one after the event of the
Incarnation. This view is somewhat obscured in Nestorius by
his cloudy metaphysics; but it stands out sharply in Theodore
of Mopsuestia, as may be seen in the fragment of the *De Incarnatione* cited by Mr. Hodgson on page 408. If you want psychology, here you have it; the Fathers at Chalcedon did not want
psychology of this brand.

[7] Ἕνωσις καθ᾽ ὑπόστασιν or ὑποστατική.

the sense that its bearer could be called *a* man instead of merely man.

Linguistically, on this point, Cyril triumphed, and hypostatic union, despite its tinge of very dubious metaphysics, has been accepted as the orthodox phrase for the mystery of the Incarnation. But several questions may well be raised as to the status of the defeated party, and indeed have been raised with no little vehemence: (1) Were the real views of Nestorius, or only a fanciful Nestorianism, condemned by the third general council at Ephesus? (2) Was Nestorius justified and rehabilitated by the later councils? (3) Did Nestorius offer a rationally sound solution of that thing truly paradoxical, the Incarnation?

To the first of these questions I do not care to answer. The Council of Ephesus has no decent claim to be called ecumenical, and its decisions dogmatically are obscure, though its condemnation of the man Nestorius, the enemy of Cyril, was sharp enough. To the second question I think we must respond both yes and no. If the reader will look back to the great Definition of Chalcedon, he will find that the contentious word Theotokos is there sustained in deference to Cyril, but with its sting so drawn by the added phrase "as touching the manhood" that it would have been acceptable to Nestorius; and so far the Antiochene was vindicated. But certainly no candid critic can interpret the last clauses of the document into anything short of a clear repudiation of the peculiar doctrine of Nestorius as to a prosôpic union. The Definition states that two distinct natures concur into, or under, one person and one subsistence, thus identifying the terms *prosôpon* and *hypostasis* which Nestorius had sought to distinguish. In the most essential point Nestorianism was as definitely condemned at the fourth council as Nestorius had been at the third.

But the matter is not so plain when we come to the next two councils, both held in Constantinople, and both, though with doubtful propriety, recognized as ecumenical. Here we enter the region of obscure and disputable psychology, turning on the relation of personality to will. In the effort to clarify his theory of the personal unification Nestorius argued as follows:

"Since then in a manner unsearchable He condescended in all things with an incomparable condescension, (here) again was shown one purpose, one will, one mind—not to be distinguished or divided—as though in One (being). And in might and in authority and in judgement—in all things He (the Man) was partaker with God inseparably; (acting) as though from One, with one discrimination and choice of both; in such a way that in things human He should not, as human, possess aught as (peculiarly) His own, but that the will of God should be His will."[8]

Here surely, if words mean anything, we have an attempt to explain the unification of two persons as the result of an ultimate harmonization of two wills. Now in opposition to just such a view the fifth council virtually, though perhaps not explicitly, proclaimed that Christ possessed only one will and that divine. But the sixth council, whose decree has been accepted in the East and West as orthodox, established the doctrine of two wills acting in such harmony as to appear to be one (Dyotheletism) in language which agrees on this point substantially with the passage just quoted from Nestorius. In the matter of orthodoxy then we must, I fear, come to this rather unsatisfactory conclusion. By the Definition of

[8] Bethune-Baker, *Op. Cit.*, 132. The same passage is found, in a slightly different version, in Driver and Hodgson, p. 70. Elsewhere, p. 5, Nestorius makes love the source of the prosôpic union.

Chalcedon, and so far as this remains the un-
shaken foundation of the Church, Nestorius
was a heretic, and Nestorianism is heresy. By
the words of the sixth council that decision still
abides intact, in so far as psychologically we are
able to discriminate between personality and
will; but if in our simplicity we refuse to follow so refined a distinction, then, by the standard of Chalcedon, both the Dyotheletism of
Nestorius and the Dyotheletism of the sixth
council are as heretical as is the abhorred doctrine of two persons coalescing into one.

And in this judgement we see the answer to
the third question raised above, viz. whether
Nestorius was successful in discovering a rational solution of the difficulties inherent in the
Incarnation. To me at least the only result of
his laborious subtleties was to render the under-
lying paradox of faith more paradoxical, or, if
you will, to convert a paradox into an absurdity.
It is paradox to assert that Christ was one
hypostasis, or person, with two natures; it becomes an absurdity when subjected to the
scrutiny of a rationalizing analysis. We may
recognize the service of the Antiochenes in resisting the insidious currents of docetism em-
anating from Alexandria; but we must con-

clude that, if Nestorianism had run its course without hindrance, Christianity would have shattered itself on the rocks of an impossible psychology.[9]

In the Nestorianism condemned by the orthodox Fathers, whether or not with injustice to its reputed author, we see the consummation of that humanitarian strain which, beginning with the Judaizers of the Apostolic Church, came to a head in the theology of Arius, and then renewed its vigour in the Christology of Antioch. This was the Scylla of the ecclesiastical voyage. On the other side lay the Charybdis of those views of Christ which in one way or another slurred over the reality or completeness of his human nature, and which, strange as it may sound, have in the long run proved the more alluring temptation to faith. Judaism and docetism, Arianism and Sabellianism, Nestorianism and Monophysitism:

---

[9] It is a matter curious in itself and not irrelevant to our thesis, that the school of Antioch was brought into sympathetic relations with Pelagianism, the single heresy originated by the Latin mind which turned on a philosophical problem. It is significant also that the error of Pelagius lay in giving too much weight to the human will in the process of salvation at the expense of divine grace, whereas the Antiochenes were interested primarily in the nature of the Saviour himself.

Upborne to heaven on ocean's curving swell,
Then with the wave sunk down to nether hell,
Thrice we behold the stars o'erblown with spume,
Thrice in deep caverns hear the waters boom.

The suppression of the Apollinarian sects had been something like the work of a physician who cures external symptoms by driving a disease inwards. The mass of those convicted were brought to allegiance to the orthodox profession, but avenged themselves by carrying the leaven of their error into the body of the Church. And out of that fermentation grew the far more dangerous heresy called Monophysitism from its insistence on one nature in Christ, or Eutychianism from the name of its chief exponent.

It is a question how far Cyril of Alexandria, in his opposition to Nestorius, had already gone in this direction, and, needless to say, the very fact that he has been canonized by the Church as one of the bulwarks of orthodoxy makes it almost obligatory upon scholars of a certain type to treat him as a heretic, or, from a different point of view, to maintain that he should have been so treated by the Church,—one or the other, the saint or the orthodox community must be wrong. Fortunately for me, I have no call to track the sanctified Alexandrian through all the anfractuosities of his path. Certainly as a politician he was crooked; as a theologian he was at once inconsistent in his use of terms and insolent to those who differed from him. His politics I abandon to his critics; his theology I am inclined to regard as substantially sound despite the confusion of his language. The trouble sprang from that mischievous word "nature," which has always been, and still is, the source of endless ambiguities and misunderstandings. Both the Antiochenes and the Apollinarians had failed to distinguish clearly between nature and personality, with what results we have seen; and in his contest with Nestorius the Alexandrian patriarch fell into the same ambush, although the Cappadocians had now pretty well fixed the usage of the two treacherous terms. To this extent, in his language at least, he might appear to be in agreement with Apollinarius. But there was this difference. When brought to book, Cyril admitted his fault and adopted the orthodox vocabulary. At bottom, though undoubtedly the temptation of his intellect was towards Monophysitism, his stronger desire was to stand square with the great tradition.

Cyril ended his stormy and somewhat devious career in 444, and the Alexandrian church passed into the hands of Dioscorus, who, if the evidence brought forward at Chalcedon can be credited, came as near to divorcing morality from faith as did any man in that scandalous age. In theory he carried the Christological views of his predecessor to their bitter conclusion, refusing to draw back at the point where one-sided orthodoxy passed into open heresy; but in practice he tried to bring infamy upon the name of Cyril and confiscated his property —the latter action being perhaps the cause of the former. The condition of the Church was now something like that of ancient Gaul—*ecclesia est omnis divisa in partes tres*. With Dioscorus and his suffragans stood Egypt and Palestine and Thrace; against him and inclining to the Nestorian opinion were arrayed Syria and a large section of Asia Minor, the Oriental party as it is called; while pitted against both sides Rome had with her virtually the whole of the West under the headship of Pope Leo.

The focus of trouble was Constantinople, where the Emperor, Theodosius II, sympathized with the policy of Dioscorus, while his archbishop, Flavian, fearing the encroachments

of the Alexandrian despot and hating the
Egyptian theology, allied himself with Leo,
who in turn was ready enough to extend the
authority of Rome into the East. The religion
of Jesus, under the sway of a fantastic metaphysic wielded by a degenerate people, had
come to resemble a witches' cauldron in which
all unclean things were boiling, and of which
the stench was offending the heavens. Among
the dancers around that hell-brew were the
monks, who by this time swarmed over the
lands, and of all the monks, those in the country
about Constantinople were perhaps the most
fanatical, and of these the leader was Eutyches,
archimandrite of a large monastery outside the
walls of the city. This man, whose life belied
the good omen of his name, had been of the
party of Cyril in the conflict between the two
metropolitan sees, and now naturally sided with
Dioscorus. Though in no sense a trained theologian, he held pronounced views on the question of the two natures, and had even been suspected of Apollinarianism in his opposition to
his former diocesan, Nestorius. Now, under
Flavian, he was accused of heresy and summoned to appear before a synod at Constantinople in 448. The test applied to him was, so to

speak, the reverse of that used at Nicea. There the issue had been whether Christ was of the same substance (*homoousios*) with the Father; here it was whether Christ, in the flesh, should be held to be also of the same substance with us men. Brought to bay, Eutyches finally admitted that, according to his confession, there might have been two natures before the union, but that after the union the human nature of Christ was so entirely absorbed into the divine as to leave only one nature, as there was only one person. In other words, barring the dubious phrase "before the union," he stood out as an avowed Monophysite, and to support his position cited the language of Cyril and writings of Apollinarian origin fraudulently attributed to Athanasius. Thus, through the opening offered by a confusion of terms, the old taint of docetism came once more to the surface, in more virulent form, threatening to reduce the human Jesus of the Gospels to a fabulous figure of legend and to convert the dogma of the Incarnation into a mere illusion. Eutyches was condemned and deposed, to the dismay of the Emperor, who forthwith appointed a commission to look into the proceedings.

At this point the western Church entered the dispute, and Leo, to whom both parties had appealed, wrote his famous Tome, in which, following the curt language of Tertullian, and making short shrift of the subtleties of both Nestorians and Monophysites, he declared Christ to be "two natures in one person." Nevertheless a synod was held at Ephesus (not to be confounded with the third ecumenical council), at which Dioscorus and his monks, with the countenance of the Emperor, acquitted Eutyches and in turn deposed Flavian. Alexandria was victorious, but by methods so violent and disgraceful that Leo pronounced the assembly at Ephesus no true council but a gathering of robbers (*latrocinium*), by which name it has come down to history. The situation was plainly intolerable. The triumph of the Nicene Faith over those who in one way or another rejected the divinity of Christ would seem to have resulted in the no less detrimental heresy of denying to him any true manhood. Leo, with the concurrence of the western court, wrote to Theodosius, urging that nothing further should be done until the whole controversy might be considered and settled by a general council to be convened at Rome. Theodosius replied that

there was no need of such a council, since a
settlement had been reached already and the
East was at peace with itself. And then, on the
twenty-eighth of July 450, Theodosius was
killed by a fall from his horse, his sister Pulcheria, with her husband Marcian, reigned in
his stead, and the whole situation was changed.
But for that accident, providential in the eyes
of many students of history, it is probable that
the East and the West would have fallen asunder before the foundation of the faith had been
laid, and there would have been no standard
of orthodoxy for the world, no possibility of the
Catholic Church for which the hearts of men
are still yearning.

Pulcheria and Marcian were clear-sighted
and orthodox. Somewhat to the chagrin of the
Pope, who saw the power of decision slipping
from his hands, they summoned a general council, not in Italy as Leo had wished, but under
the shadow of their own capital. Hither then,
to Chalcedon in Bithynia, came the great con-
course of bishops in October of the year 451.
Envoys of Leo were sent from Rome, provided
with copies of the papal Tome and fully instructed as to their procedure; Dioscorus was
there, with his adherents about him, seated at

the right of the tribunal. Altogether there were present, either in person or by proxy, six hundred and thirty bishops, the largest convocation the Church had yet known. In the main, the proceedings seem to have been harmonious. At the first session Flavian was justified, and Dioscorus with the others responsible for the Latrocinium was deposed. "A just sentence," the assembly exclaimed, and as it adjourned, the hour being now late, raised for the first time recorded in history the liturgical anthem of the *Trisagion*: "Holy God, holy and strong, holy and immortal, have mercy upon us!" The acts of this fourth council, the last which can be properly called ecumenical, should be to us a much-needed reminder that, beside the princely prelates who were the children of the unholy union of State and Church and whose unlovely ambitions fill the pages of history, there was a vast body of priests and laymen who clung to the simplicity of the faith and were the true inheritors and transmitters of Christianity.

In the matter of doctrine the fourth council took as the basis of orthodoxy the Nicene Faith, along with which it accepted the so-called Nicene Creed, Cyril's second letter to Nestorius, his letter to John of Antioch, and the Tome of

Leo. "The present synod," said the papal delegate in reply to a question of the presiding magistrates, "holds this Faith; and can neither add thereto, nor take therefrom"; to which statement the bishops cried out their assent: "So we all believe! So were we baptized! So we baptize!" And then at the end, though after much debate, they confirmed with acclaim the famous *Definition of the Faith,* in the form in which we now have it.

As the assembled bishops were careful to assert, this Definition introduced nothing new but was merely supplementary to the Nicene formula, so that the two documents make together what may be called the Niceo-Chalcedonian Profession of Faith. Now, as I have said before, the immediate impression of a modern reader who lights by chance upon this formulation of the Christian belief is likely to be a feeling of repulsion. And undoubtedly there is cause for regret that the exigencies of the times compelled the Fathers to adopt so harsh—let us even say so precise—a terminology for that which might better have been left in fluid form as it was given to the world in the Gospels. No believer of today can resent this necessity of definition more deeply than did the

wiser theologians of antiquity. But I think that
if the Profession be read again with the history
of the preceding and succeeding heresies in
mind, and with full understanding of what
these aberrations mean,—I think then that this
feeling of repulsion will give place to wonder
and admiration. For let us consider briefly, by
way of recapitulation, what had happened.

To these adherents of the new religion had
come by written and oral tradition the story of
a man who lived and spoke as other men, yet
who claimed to be a prophet and something
more than a prophet,—a man who in one breath
summoned the world to allegiance to God and
to himself, whose message fell upon their ears
through all the wild mummery and frantic inventions of that superstitious age with clear
and commanding simplicity:

"God is a Spirit, and they that worship him
must worship him in spirit and in truth."

"Blessed are the pure in heart, for they shall
see God."

"He that hath seen me hath seen the Father."

"Blessed are the poor in spirit, for theirs is
the kingdom of heaven."

"And I, if I be lifted up from the earth, will
draw all men unto me."

"Be of good cheer, I have overcome the world."

"Come unto me."

These were the words of Jesus himself, and those who now heard them knew also that the heralds of the new gospel declared him to be "the Son of God with power, according to the spirit of holiness, by the resurrection from the dead," to be even the Word of God, verily the Word who was God. This was the tradition, and, by virtue of the answering logos within his own breast, he who heard it believed that its source was in the everlasting fountain of veracity. It was a voice which, like the voice that came to Socrates in gaol, he was bound to follow, because, amid the din of a thousand conflicting arguments, it alone promised the true deliverance: "Such words I seem to hear, as the mystic worshippers seem to hear the piping of flutes; and the sound of this voice so murmurs in my ears that I can hear no other."[10]

Nor was this inner conviction left without confirmation. This event of the gospel had occurred in an obscure corner of the earth amidst a despised people, and those who went forth to

[10] *Crito*, 54D.—Cf. *ibid.*, 46B: Τῷ λόγῳ ὃς ἄν μοι λογιζομένῳ βέλτιστος φαίνηται.

preach it came with no skill in dialectic, no
grace of utterance, no influence of position;
yet the glory of the bare message had so in-
flamed the imagination of men that they were
ready to adopt a totally new manner of life and
for their love of Christ to laugh in the face of
obloquy and torture. Before this faith the ancient wisdom of the world had, as it were, folded
its cloak about it and stalked away into the shadows of night; while the secular pride of power
had at first threatened, and then wavered, and
at last bowed its crowned head. The miracle of
history was happening, not in the dim past, but
under the very observation of the believers. It is
not strange that their faith was ardent and in-
vincible.

Now it must not be supposed that the heresies which arose in quick succession were devised
with the least intention to diminish the honour
of the new religion. On the contrary, the heresiarchs—at least the better minds among them,
and as such the more dangerous—were men who
aimed at fortifying the dogma of the Incarnation by expounding it in a manner consonant
with the laws of logic. To accomplish this task
they took, as I have attempted to show, either
one or the other of two opposite courses: the

way of docetism which emphasized the Godhead of Christ to the overshadowing of his manhood, or the way of the Ebionites or Judaizers,
as they were primarily called, who clung to the
manhood of Christ at the cost of his divinity.
Now in one sense it cannot be said that their
labour, however futile its end, was a mere waste
of spirit. On its positive side each of these sects
laid hold of a necessary aspect of the truth and
developed it to the utmost, so that the sum of
all their contentions was to bring out the infinite riches of the faith. From that point of
view there would seem to be some lack of intelligence in the common impatience of modern
scholars with the whole range of Greek theology as "barren" and "bankrupt."

But individually, and on its negative side,
each of these major heresies was a blow levelled
at the very spirit of faith and worship which it
sought to elucidate, in the one case by slurring
over the function of the Saviour as representative of the human race, in the other case by
clouding his mission as revealer of God. More
than that—and the point I would now make
would be clearer if the innumerable subsidiary
heresies had been brought into our survey—in
the period under consideration every possible

means of reconciling the Incarnation, that "thing truly paradoxical" as Athanasius admitted, with the monistic demands of reason had been tried, and all had ended in logical confusion and moral disaster. The time had come to call a halt. The constructive work of the Greek intelligence had been accomplished, once for all; the centrifugal force of the Greek character threatened to dissipate religion into endless factions. There was needed just such a statement of orthodoxy as that provided by Chalcedon—a formula which, in hard, precise, immitigable terms, should set a check upon the claims of reason to extend the faith in one direction to the exclusion of the other. It had come to this pass: either the central fact of Christianity had to be abandoned, or such claims of reason had to be transcended. You may rationally reverence Christ as an inspired man (at least you may if you do not inquire too curiously into the meaning of inspiration), or you may rationally (if it so pleases your fancy) dissolve an event of history into a fiction of the mythopoeic imagination, and to one or the other of these extremes all the heresies were inevitably sloping; you cannot rationally worship the incarnate Saviour, as both the orthodox and all but the most intransigent heretics understand worship.

Such an admission may be painful, even humiliating. But, after all, the dogma of the Incarnation is no whit more irrational than the dualism which meets us at every turn of our inquiry into the nature of things,—*e.g.* than the incomprehensible junction of body and mind with which every act of our life makes us familiar, and against which the endeavours of a rationalizing psychology break down invariably in wanton disregard of facts or in gross abuse of logic.[11] The analogy, I may add, was clearly perceived by the theologians of the faith fifteen hundred years ago, and was even embodied in the creed improperly attributed to Athanasius: *"As the reasonable soul and flesh is one man, so God and Man is one Christ."* However our pride of intellect may rebel, there can be no intelligent attitude towards the greater problems of existence until we have learned that reason, though it may be the pragmatic guide of conduct, is not the source of knowledge or even the final test of truth. The question put to the soul of each man is not whether the primary tenet

11 This argument I have developed in the first chapter of *The Christ of the New Testament.*

of Christianity has the kind of consistency demanded by logic, but whether it corresponds
with the lessons and surest intuitions of spiritual experience.

CHAPTER IX

CHALCEDON AND THE GREEK TRADITION

In the preceding chapter we have seen what the state of the world was when the Council met at Chalcedon, and under what compulsion the Fathers issued the famous Definition of the Faith. Rent by contending factions, harassed and outwearied, the leaders of the Church thought less, one suspects, of formulating a doctrine than of putting a quietus upon disputation. Their mood was to cry out "a plague o' both your houses"; but in their despair they builded more wisely than they knew. To us, looking back with calmer mind and wider experience, the significance of the Definition may be resumed under a few heads.

I. The Fathers were careful to assert that they were not promulgating a new creed, but were simply clarifying what at Nicea had been left at loose ends. The Definition of Chalcedon is properly a supplement to the Nicene Faith and forms with it a single Profession.

II. Though the later document is called a definition, it makes no attempt to define psychologically or philosophically the various terms employed. It is not metaphysical, but the negation of metaphysics. In this respect it stands at the close of an era and marks the turning point of theology. Shortly after Chalcedon the scholasticism of Aristotelian logic, hitherto the weapon of heresy, was definitely introduced into orthodox theology by Leontius of Byzantium with his attempt to explain the Incarnation as a kind of mechanical *enhypostasis*.[1] And, as we have seen, the fifth and sixth general councils followed this false guidance in their efforts to deal psychologically with the same mystery. As a consequence the fifth council virtually repeated the error which had been condemned for heresy in Apollinarius and Eutyches, while the sixth council quite frankly adopted views which had driven Nestorius into exile. This is not to say that the fifth council was wrong in seeing only one will in Christ because the sixth council saw two wills in him, or

[1] For an account of this theory and an attempt to justify it, see *A Study in Christology*, by Herbert M. Relton.

that the sixth was wrong in decreeing the dogma of two wills because the fifth admitted (virtually) only one will; it means rather that any such analysis of the Incarnation is bound to lead into exaggerations that can barely be distinguished from heresy. It means that the Fathers at Chalcedon were altogether wise in restricting their statement to such general terms as personality and nature, and that to enter into the complicated and utterly obscure relation of personality to the will is to invite certain confusion and probable disaster. That way lay the devious course of medieval scholasticism, the top-heavy metaphysics of Thomas Aquinas, and the Nessus shirt of irrational rationalism from which Rome can escape only by a miracle.[2] Against that *via dolorosa* of the

[2] I do not for a moment deny the intellectual acumen of the greater schoolmen or the monumental achievement of St. Thomas, but I do assert that their method of dealing with the truths of religion is based on an essential fallacy and has proved embarrassing to Christianity. And so, despite all her practical wisdom and the glory of her long tradition and her stalwart adherence to the fundamental dogmas of antiquity, I feel that Rome has committed herself philosophically to an impossible position. The very inertia of the eastern Church since her decline in the fifth century may in the end turn out to her advantage. To see the utter débâcle of the Orient and the withdrawal of the last spark of Hellenic inspiration after Chrysostom, one need only read such a work as *The Chronicle of Zachariah of Mitylene* (translated by F. J. Hamilton and E. W. Brooks). The revived Greek Church of today joins hands with antiquity across a huge gape; and it is curious to find the

intellect there is an admirable protest in a document attributed in our manuscripts to Athanasius: "From asking how and in what way, men fell into disbelief. . . . What need have we to question and split words? It is better to believe and adore and worship in silence. I know him truly God from heaven, passionless; I know him from the seed of David according to the flesh, man from the earth subjected to passion. I do not ask how the same person is subject to passion and passionless, how he is God and how man, lest, being overcurious in regard to the how and questioning the manner, I fall from the good set before me."[3]

III. To the absence of any attempt to define its terms in the so-called Definition must be attributed, in part at least, the obstinate inability of certain modern critics to comprehend its import. Thus Harnack complains that by conceding so much to the Nestorian dualism of natures the council failed to reach any clear

modern theologians of Athens quoting the Fathers of the third and fourth centuries quite as if they were contemporaries.

[3] From the *Quod Unus Sit Christus*, which Lietzmann includes among the works of Apollinarius (p. 294). There are passages in the document which make this attribution plausible, but at least the words here quoted are fully in the spirit and according to the practice of Athanasius. And certainly the tragedy of Apollinarius' life springs from his failure to obey such a precept.

and logical conception of the Incarnation:
"The real mystery was thus shoved aside by a
pseudo-mystery which in truth no longer permitted theology to advance to the thought of
the actual and perfect union." Against this view
Loofs, the other outstanding historian of dogma
in Germany, holds that the fault of the council
was in admitting any compromise with the
monophysite tendency of Cyril: "Only by returning to the lines of the Antiochian theology,
. . . can we arrive at an understanding of the
Johannine saying, 'the Word was made flesh,'
which is in harmony with the New Testament
and avoids theological and rational impossibilities."[4] And, combining the two causes of complaint, Dorner criticises the Chalcedonian position with impartial contempt: "All that that
council really did was to decide on two negations,—the negation of the unity of nature, and
that of the duality of persons." Precisely. Only
we should remember that in theology, as in
grammar, two negations may make a positive.
The equivalent of Dorner's criticism would be
exactly this: All that that council really did was
to decide on two affirmations—the affirmation

[4] Quoted by Dr. A. C. Headlam in his preface to Relton's book
cited above. Bishop Gore, in the fourth chapter of his *Bampton
Lectures,* has the wisest comment on Chalcedon known to me.

of the duality of natures, and that of the unity of person. That was all, and by the mercy of Providence there was no more. The language of the Definition, bristling to the eye with theological terms, is like a prickly hedge set about a fair garden; what it guards within is the very simple faith with which Christianity started on its career and by which it conquered the world. And a little acquaintance with ancient and modern theology will show that the present efforts to break down the Niceo-Chalcedonian Profession are but ill-disguised repetitions of one or another of the old heresies that troubled the faithful many centuries since, and were brusquely ejected from the Church. One and all they are aiming to avoid "the thing truly paradoxical" by substituting for it some pleasant fiction of the reason; and they will suffer the same ignominious fate as their predecessors—or, triumphing, they will see the religion of worship fade away into a pure agnosticism or a bloodless mysticism.

IV. The utterance of Chalcedon, properly understood, may be regarded as the consummation of the Hebrew tradition, in so far as the message of the prophets was revived by Jesus Christ and made into a new religion through his

assumption to himself of its latent significance.
This was the theme of the preceding volume of
this series.

V. And as Chalcedon was the fulfilment of
Hebrew prophecy, so was it also the consummation of Greek philosophy. And here again,
as at almost every step of our progress, it is
necessary to clear away certain obstacles of
prejudice before the truth can be seen. On
many points Harnack and Loofs, to name the
two most influential of the German historians
of dogma, are in disagreement, but in one thing
they concur: in holding that the Definiton of
Chalcedon was essentially western in origin,
and was forced upon the unwilling Orient by
the high hand of authority. That is an error
only the more misleading for the half-truth it
contains. The question before the bishops at the
fourth council was one which had occupied the
Greek mind continually from the very beginning of Christianity, and which of late years
had thrown the eastern Church into a turmoil
of dissension; whereas among the Latins the
doctrine of the Incarnation had simply been
taken over as it were on trust. So far as the
Occident thought independently and raised new
questions, it was in the sphere of Church disci-

pline and organization, and over the problem of the part played by the human will in the process of salvation. Donatism and Pelagianism were the two major heresies that originated in the West, and the two corresponding masters of the Church were Cyprian and Augustine. In the central dogma of the faith the Roman mind created nothing philosophically or theologically; but by virtue of its legal habitude and its sense of authority it did perform one important service: it gave expression to that dogma in the terse practical form of a decree. To Tertullian we owe the sharp concentration of Greek thought in the forensic formula *non confusum sed conjunctum in una persona,* and to Leo in the main must be accredited the event that at Chalcedon the perplexed Fathers turned to this formula as something fixed, to which they could cling for refuge from the restless fluidity of their own inventions. Such was the function of Rome in those days. The synods of Nicea and of Chalcedon might have lost themselves in infinite quibblings were it not for the check imposed by the authority of Latin legalism. Nevertheless, though formulation is much, the idea formulated is more; and in that sense it is correct to say that Chalcedon was the outcome

of centuries of speculation over the central
problem of Christian faith among a people who,
however degenerate in many respects, were yet
the inheritors of the language and philosophy
of Hellas.

VI. But Chalcedon was the consummation
of the Greek tradition in a still deeper sense. At
the root of Plato's philosophy lies the perception of a dividing cleft between our experience
of that which comes to us as stable, eternal,
immutable, unitary, possessible, joyous, peace-
giving, somehow right, and our experience of
that which comes to us as shifting, ephemeral,
transient, various, elusive, mingled of pleasure
and pain, distracting, somehow weighted with
evil; on one side our knowledge of Ideas, on the
other side our opinions of phenomena. Yet this
world of our experience is still one world, a cosmos, though it combines within itself, and without confusion, two utterly disparate natures;
and I who live in this double experience am still
one person. This to Plato was the "thing truly
paradoxical" which puzzled him and drove him
ever on and on to traverse "many ways in the
wanderings of thought."

At one moment in his career he seems to have
believed that he had found a rational solution

of the problem, or at least that he could state it
in such a manner as to enable the mind to rest
comfortably in pure philosophical contemplation,—at that moment in the composition of
The Republic when there came to him the great
vision of the Idea of the Good riding in the
spiritual sky as the sun traverses the physical
heavens, the source of knowledge and joy to all
souls who are capable of bearing its supernal
light, the cause of being to all objects which
exist through desire of participating in its absolute reality. To many students of the dialogues this appears to be the utmost reach of
Plato's thought, the summit from which he
declined in later years to an almost senile acceptance of popular superstitions. I cannot consent to such a view. I see rather that Plato
became aware of the serious insufficiency of his
purely philosophical theory of Ideas, and in the
later modifications of, or more precisely additions to, the theory was anticipating the
double criticism directed upon it by Aristotle.
What, he appears to have asked himself, as
Aristotle did actually ask, is the dynamic bond
between Ideas and phenomena? How are the
universal forms contained in particular objects
without forfeiting their distinct character?

Where is the source of life and the principle of creation in Ideas as inanimate things? How does the Idea of the Good act as the cause of being? And again, on the practical, ethical side, is this pure philosophy of Ideas capable of satisfying the innate craving of the heart for happiness? On this second aspect of the problem we must pause for a moment, since in it are to be found, I think, the key to much misunderstanding of Platonism itself and the line of development from the philosophy of the Academy to the theology of the Church.

The question raised and discussed in *The Republic* is this, whether it is really better under all circumstances to be just than unjust,— a question that appears simple enough on the surface, but that opens into depth beneath depth if attentively examined. In the first place we must determine precisely what justice is, in other words, we must discover the Idea of justice (or of the Good, since justice here stands for goodness in the generic sense). Then, having done this, we must demonstrate to our complete satisfaction that he who possesses this Idea and moulds his life upon it will inevitably be happy. To that end the young interlocutors of Socrates, at the beginning of the second

book of the dialogue, lay down this hypothetical
case: let us take a man absolutely just, who yet
bears the reputation of injustice and suffers
accordingly the severest penalties of crime, with
no hope of release and no expectation of re-
ward in the honours and blessings of this life;
and let us suppose further that there are no
gods, or that, if the gods exist, they pay no heed
to the doings of men, so that our just man can
look for no vindication and recompense in a life
to come. Will such a one, though tortured on
the rack and crucified, though deprived of all
present pleasures and future hope, still be the
happy man by reason of the sole possession of
justice in his heart? Yes, replies Socrates with
unwavering faith; and thereupon undertakes
to show what justice is, and to demonstrate by
appeal to history and psychology that the just
man is happy and the unjust man correspond-
ingly miserable.

The exposition of the nature of justice, cul-
minating in the glorification of the Idea of the
Good, we may pass by for the present. The
point I would make is that nowhere in the
eighth and ninth books, in which he exemplifies
the effect of justice and injustice in the State
and in the life of the individual, that not once

does Plato, or his mouthpiece Socrates, really
face the hypothesis laid down in the second
book. He does demonstrate with all the per-
suasiveness of masterly art that, under normal
conditions, the just State prospers and the just
man is happy. He does make us see, by the
memorable image of the triple beast within us,
how the evil man, though he be reputed good
and bear off all the prizes of the world, is still a
wretched and distracted creature. He brings
before us the nobility of the joys that belong to
one who has weaned his mind from the pursuit
of illusory pleasures to the contemplation of
everlasting realities, and, with a humorous turn
to mathematics, calculates that the life of the
true philosopher, passed as it were in the world
of Ideas, is seven hundred and twenty-nine
times pleasanter than that of the tyrant who has
captured all the powers and treasures of this
earth. All this is magnificently done. Nevertheless the argument goes about and around, and
never meets squarely the conditions laid down
at the beginning,—never meets them at all until
they are virtually withdrawn. So Socrates declares towards the close of the dialogue: "Such
then must be our opinion in regard to the just
man, that, even though he be in poverty or

sickness or any other seeming evil, these things
will somehow end for him in good, either in this
life or after death." But this *after death* was the
very point carefully excluded by the hypothesis; and this summary conclusion follows, and
could only follow, a plea for that immortality
of the soul which was voluntarily surrendered
as non-essential to the thesis of pure philosophy.

The fact is that Plato's evasion of the issue
raised by himself tacitly anticipates the verdict
pronounced by Aristotle: "Those who say that
a man on the rack . . . is happy, if he be good,
either wittingly or unwittingly speak nonsense."[5] How can it be otherwise? How indeed
can there be any question of justice or the effect
of justice, how can there be any moral philosophy, in a world so constituted that the good
man, for no fault of his own, with no prospect
of release, with no hope of a future life, with no
lesson to learn, with nothing but the blank and
hideous present, may be subjected to killing
torment? In such a world is it anything but
mockery to talk about eternal Ideas and the
blessedness of dwelling in their contemplation?
And so suddenly, in the tenth book, Socrates

[5] *Eth. Nic.*, VII, xiii, 3.

makes his appeal to the belief in the immortality of the soul, and in the providence of a God
who so governs the world that in the long lapse
of time the justice of circumstances shall correspond with our inner sense of what is just,
while righteousness and happiness become truly
and fully synonymous.

There is, I admit, something startling, almost disconcerting, in this view of *The Republic*.[6] Did Plato really believe, as he seems to
assume, that the unmitigated hypothesis of the
second book was established by the illustrations
given in the eighth and ninth books? Did it
escape his notice that the religious concession of
the tenth book is not, as he declares it to be, a
mere addition to, or confirmation of, the argument of the earlier books, but is virtually an
admission that his great philosophical thesis, if
taken literally, was untenable and at bottom
meaningless? I will not presume to answer this
question; but I can see that what lies behind the
apparent opposition of the two theses of the
dialogue is a shift in interest, or emphasis, rela-
tively to the two elements, morality and otherworldliness, which enter into religious philos-

6 This view of *The Republic* had not occurred to me when I
wrote *The Religion of Plato*, nor do I recall any critic of Plato
who has really faced the question here raised.

ophy. It is not that the element of otherworldliness had been rejected from his philosophical
hypothesis, for the conception of justice there
adopted leads straight on to the supreme vision
of the Idea of the Good. Nor was the need of
morality overlooked in the theology and mythology of the tenth book; even here goodness remains the primary and indispensable source of
all true religion. The change came rather with
a perception of the inadequacy of the otherworld as conceived for the purpose of his
hypothesis, and with the new significance imparted to it by a fuller recognition of the rôle
therein of what we call personality. The hypothesis of a soul assured of happiness here and
now by participation somehow in a world of
inanimate Ideas, with no thought of anything
beyond, simply did not work out. Unless philosophy were to prove a mockery, it needed to
be supplemented by an extension of the soul's
life beyond these barriers of time and by the
addition of God, or the gods, to the Ideal
sphere. I think that Plato never for an instant
really doubted the immortality of the human
soul or the existence of God, and that his paradoxical hypothesis of *The Republic* was a kind
of defiance thrown out to the sceptical material-

ist, as though he were saying: If life may be lived nobly (as it always can) and happily (as under normal circumstances it can) with no faith in immortality or divine Providence, then what should be the nobility and happiness and security of our state with that faith granted? I think that for the moment he was not aware of the full scope of that condition "under normal circumstances," and did not see how it reduced philosophy, severed from faith, to a beautiful but vain illusion.

In this way I explain the position of Plato in his later dialogues. There is no return to his hypothesis of the all-sufficient present for the human soul, while his conception of the otherworld undergoes a profound alteration. In the *Timaeus* the doctrine of Ideas is retained, but now, as *things,* they are held to be purely passive and inert, while the creative energy formerly ascribed to them is transferred to God, who fashions this world of phenomena by taking them for His model of perfection. And in the tenth book of the *Laws* Plato explicitly repudiates the hypothesis of *The Republic* in order to base morality more directly on the obedient relation of the human soul to God. Platonism then, as it left the master's hand, was

a theistic faith based on a philosophy of una-
bashed dualism. On the higher side stands God,
whose home and life, so to speak, are in the pure
Ideal realm, and who, as Creator, fashions to
the end of some divine and beneficent purpose
this world of phenomena and the souls who
dwell therein. On the other side is seen dimly,
through the night of our ignorance, the lower
cause (if cause it may be named which is the
very negation of causality), the still unsubdued,
perhaps forever rebellious, Necessity, sitting
like Milton's Sin at the mouth of Hell,—the
unaccountable residue of random change and
unchecked desire with all their attendant brood
of mischiefs, the sprawling infinity which in-
terposes between God and His creative will,
thwarting the realization of ideal order and
limiting the imposition of law upon this middle
and mingled sphere of things as they are.

This, the dualism of the *Timaeus* and the
Laws, which is not so much an innovation with
Plato as a development of the religious intuition of his youth which only for a while was
threatened with eclipse,—this I take to be the
core of the Greek tradition. But, as I have attempted to show elsewhere, it was overlaid and
surrounded by a succession of Hellenistic phil-

osophies which essayed, each on its own lines, to explain the nature of things by a scheme of monistic rationalism. For this reason I hold that the true heir of the Academy was not the Neoplatonism of Plotinus and Porphyry and Proclus, but the Christian philosophy of the great Alexandrians and Cappadocians.

VII. Nor is it really difficult to follow the line of succession. The Stoics had merged together the creative will of God and the Ideas in their theory of an immanent logos—immanent, that is to say, as abiding within and permeating this material world, which is itself only a slackened and sluggish manifestation of the same primitive element. The logos, as the guiding and governing force within its own evolution, might be regarded as spiritual or material, personal or mechanistic, by the individual Stoic in accordance with his mood; but to any consistent thinker it resolved itself into the equivalent of our modern scientific conception of absolute, unconscious, self-sufficient Law—surely, if taken literally, about the most incomprehensible and untenable theory of the world ever promulgated. Then suddenly the notion was thrown out that this Logos, so far from being an immanent mechanical Law, was very personal indeed, was in fact the transcendent Son of God who had made himself known to men by an actual epiphany in human form, and this among the despised people of Palestine and in fulfilment of ancient Hebrew prophecy. The thought was new, amazing, overwhelmingly significant, and it took centuries of reflection, with no little clash and counter-clash of interpretation, before it could be wrought into a consistent philosophy. Unfortunately meanwhile something of the Stoic monism got rooted in Christianity and has never been thoroughly expelled. But the true development came out of the assimilation of the personal Logos with the genuine Idealism of the Academy. Where the Demiurge of Plato had fashioned the cosmos with His eye upon Ideas as the model of perfection, here in the Christian scheme the eternal pattern becomes, in a certain sense and to a certain point, identified with the Logos, through whom, hypostatized as God's eternal Wisdom and Son, God creates a world in His own likeness. The lower cause of Plato, the dark impediment of Necessity, is transformed into the Christian conception of Sin, introduced into the world by the

Fall and at the last to be redeemed by the
Incarnation.

In this new philosophy the doctrine of Ideas
is, as it were, illuminated from two sides. On
the one hand Plato had always insisted that we
know Ideas, and only them, yet he had never,
unless through an obscure myth, been able to
give a satisfactory account of the manner in
which we possess this knowledge. Now the
Word of God, as Wisdom itself and Beauty
itself and Holiness itself, as the way and the
truth and the life, had shown itself embodied in
a human character. So and so only can we really
see the Ideas, at least in our mortal state; and
so we saw them in Jesus.[7]

But if our direct knowledge of Ideas comes
to us through their personification, or, more
precisely, through the character of one who has
made them his life, this does not mean that they
have thereby lost their independent validity
and have dwindled away into mere ideas within
the mind, arbitrary evocations of thought, the
truth or falsehood of which is determined by no
correspondence with objective reality. And

[7] Hence the propriety of Gregory Nyssen's phrase (*In Bapt.
Christi*, 589в), ὁ νοητὸς Χριστός. So in the same author's *De
Beatitudinibus*, 1245c, Christ presents himself, not as righteous,
but as righteousness.

here again the Christian philosophy develops
and clarifies and vivifies the Platonic tradition.
Few things are more interesting to the student
of this period than the gradual assimilation of
the Biblical kingdom of heaven and the Platonic world of Ideas, whereby the former sheds
its temporal and national limitations and assumes the aspect of universal philosophy, while
the latter acquires a dynamic hold on the imagination and will which as pure philosophy it
could not possess. Perhaps the most perfect expression of this truth in the Fathers is the passage from Basil which I have quoted elsewhere;[8]
but the same process of mutual adaptation is
common to his contemporaries and predecessors. Gregory Nazianzen knew it well enough
and used it often.[9] The other Gregory, Basil's
brother, goes out of his way in one of his sermons on the Beatitudes[10] to liken "the earth"
promised to the meek for their inheritance to
the Ideal world seen by the soul when it stands
on the apex of the celestial vault. The whole
discourse is in substance a deliberate conflation
of the allegory of Plato's *Phaedrus* with the
kingdom of heaven as described in First Corin-

---

[8] *The Christ of the New Testament*, 85.
[9] *E.g., Funebris in Patrem*, § 3.
[10] Migne, Vol. I, col. 1209.

thians ii, 9. Gregory was here speaking the language common to his time, but he may have had more particularly in mind the elaborate use of the same allegory by Methodius, ending with the curious and striking announcement of "the restoration of the new age, when we of the Church, having been joined to the assembly of those in heaven, shall no longer consider that which is (*to on*) through the discursive reason, but shall enter into it with Christ and so contemplate it with clear vision."[11]

I think that in this retention of Ideas as at once incomprehensibly subjective and objective, in this personification of Ideas in the divine Logos, while they yet, as the impersonal law of justice and beauty, continue to be entities by their own right, and in this symbolical use of Ideas as the place and furniture, so to speak, of the spiritual life of the soul in communion with other souls and with God, we have the fine flower of Platonism blossoming after long centuries in a strange garden.

VIII. And last of all the mystery of redemption. Thinking of the division between the

---

11 Μέχριπερ ἂν τῆς ἀποκαταστάσεως τῶν καινῶν αἰώνων, εἰς τὴν ἄγυριν ἐλθοῦσα (ἡ Ἐκκλησία) κατὰ τοὺς οὐρανούς, μηκέτι δι' ἐπιστήμης κατασκέπτηται τὸ Ὄν, ἀλλὰ τρανῶς ἐποπτεύσῃ Χριστῷ συνεισβᾶσα. See *Conv. Decem. Virg.*, chaps. ii, iii, xi.

two worlds of Ideas and phenomena, and asking himself how from the perception of the fleeting appearances about us we rise to knowledge of the eternal and invisible realities, Plato had lighted upon that theory of reminiscence which to the modern mind appeals rather as poetry than as sober philosophy, yet by its author was certainly taken quite seriously. A sudden hint, he believed, of spiritual grace, caught from the glimpse of physical beauty or suggested by some act of heroism or of comely duty, awakens in the soul of the percipient memories of an earlier life when, ranging with the gods beyond this sublunary sphere, it had beheld the very paradigms of beauty and virtue and holiness, the perfect Ideas, whereof the better things of the earth are but clumsy copies. For a moment the soul is rapt, as it were, out of its heavy prison of the flesh, the veils of folly are torn away from before its eyes, and it knows the truth and breathes the air of heaven.

Now with this psychology of reminiscence combine Plato's story of the teacher whose "course was pointed out by God Himself," and who at the cost of his life went about calling upon men to concern themselves with their own souls as the one thing important, read the *Apol-*

ogy, that is to say, and consider how it represents Socrates as the very embodiment of the
salvation offered to men through the philosophy
of reminiscence, and you will see how marvellously Plato prepared the way for a religion
based on the Word made flesh, how naturally
the confluent streams of Greek speculation and
Hebrew prophecy came together, and how
properly the Greek Fathers at Chalcedon may
be said to have set their seal on the long tradition which took its rise in Athens exactly to the
year eight centuries and a half before they met.
For the repeated protest of Christ that his mission here on earth was to proclaim nothing new
but only what he had seen and heard with the
Father, is just the doctrine of reminiscence in a
fresh guise; and his further declaration that
those who had seen him had seen the Father, is
just a personification of that doctrine, the philosophy of Plato presented in such mythological
form as Plato seemed to be reaching after with
his poetical imagination. To read the allegory of
the *Phaedrus* together with the eighth chapter
of St. John, to see how the author of the Gospel, unwittingly no doubt, makes of the life and
words of Jesus a fulfilment of the Platonic

vision, is to understand the greatest moment in the history of human thought.

IX. So far the Church remained faithful to the twin tradition and to the limitations of philosophy. It slipped into metaphysics when, impressed by the significance of this new emphasis upon personality and hurried on by the precipitant urgency of the reason towards simplification, its theologians denied the dualism which is the avowed basis of the Platonic philosophy and of Christian worship, for the sake of magnifying God as the sole irresponsible cause of all things. Such a procedure may seem to be necessitated by the demands of logic, but in fact, if carried out unfalteringly, it ends at last in utter unreason.

So in regard to the upper cause in Plato's scheme of creation. It might seem that theology was adding to the glory of God by eliminating Ideas or by absorbing them entirely into the divine personality, but in truth it was thereby only depriving religion of the essential element of morality and producing conditions impossible for the spiritual life. The trail of this metaphysical nihilism can be traced straight down from antiquity, through the Fathers to the scholastic monism of Duns Scotus, who de-

rives all existence from the *fiat* of the divine
will, and makes the distinction between good
and evil to depend on an arbitrary decree.
Good is that which God, for His own irresponsible pleasure, has willed to be; if He had so
chosen to will, that which we now call evil might
have been right. And the conclusion comes with
the pure nominalism of Occam, the pupil of
Duns, who defines the divine will as a *potentia
absoluta* controlled by no reasonable consideration and accountable to no facts. As all things
flow from and hang upon the Word within
God, so all things except the infinite Person
and the finite personalities evoked by Him out
of the void are mere words, mere phantoms of
thought, with no substantial being. The circle
has come full round to the Aristotelian conception of the first cause as pure contemplation
which contemplates only contemplation. Rationalism playing with theology has reduced
the morality of religion to an empty name and
the otherworldliness of religion to a shadow
hidden beyond shadows.

And for us, what substance of reality is left
to the spiritual life? For, if one stops to reflect,
the existence of bare personalities, subject to
no law to which their will is held responsible,

and deprived of anything outside of themselves
to which their desires may be directed and from
which their happiness may be drawn, is as impossible as the existence of a breathing body in
a vacuum. The love of person to person offers
no substitute for what this spiritual nominalism
has taken away. The sympathy of soul with
soul in this our present life is conditioned by
similarity of attraction and repugnance amidst
the tides of circumstance, and by mutual understanding of the active and passive reactions of
each upon the world. And so, and not otherwise,
must we think of a life beyond the grave, if we
think of it at all. There too the society of spirits
and their communion with God cannot be severed from an impersonal, though it may be a
non-spatial, environment, a world of Ideas.
Personality as an isolated abstraction, there as
here, is a sound that signifies nothing; an absolutely spontaneous will or desire, influenced by
nothing, impeded by nothing, a pure creative-
ness, is the last and thinnest and least tenable
vapour of reason divorced from imagination.

The same sterilizing effect of metaphysics
may be observed in the treatment of Plato's
lower cause, the inner ground of imperfection
and perversion in things as they are. To the

Christian, in accordance with the increased emphasis on personality, the obscure Necessity of the *Timaeus* takes the hue and colour of sin, as if all the evils of the world could be traced back to the breaking of the soul's obedience to its Maker. In worship, in the instinctive emotions of the heart, in theology so long as it remained true to religious experience, this present world was regarded as the joint product of two causes, God's will and a thwarting power of contradiction. Mythologically the view is sound, and no harm is done by dreaming of a period of sinless perfection before the beginning of time as time is known to us. So far well. The difficulty arises when reason stepping in undertakes to use this conception of sin as an apology for a Power, at once omnipotent and absolutely benevolent, who permits His work to be marred by finite spirits whom He has endowed with free will to choose between good and evil—where yet no alternatives for choice lie before them and no temptation can be imagined. Then, juggle with words as we may, our logic falls into monstrous inconsistencies, or drives us to consider sin, in Augustine's phrase, as a *felix culpa*, a mere instrument devised for the attainment of a greater good.

These contradictions and blank impossibilities are plainly enough the penalty paid by orthodoxy for flirting with the same seductions as those which betrayed secular thought into the closed ways of Stoicism, Epicureanism, and Neoplatonism. Fortunately, beneath all the monistic divagations of theology the dualism of Plato persisted as the true philosophy of the Church in its worship and religious life. It is even more fortunate that in its Christology the progression in every direction towards the engulfing gloom of metaphysics was blocked by the Definition of Chalcedon. Here the distinction lay not between two aspects or methods of orthodox theory, but clearly between the Catholic faith on one side and heresy on the other; here the central tradition runs straight from the Academy of Athens to Jerusalem and Alexandria and Constantinople.

X. We saw that the Faith promulgated at Nicea as the test of Catholicism is different from, and anterior to, the so-called Nicene Creed which now has a place in the liturgies of both the eastern and the western Church. The relation of this liturgical creed to the Faith is one of the obscure and debated matters of ecclesiastical history, into which we need not go

at length. From the Catechetical Orations of
Cyril of Jerusalem it would appear that the
creed existed, substantially as we have it today,
in the mid-fourth century and was used in the
Palestinian church, from whence it spread over
the world. Probably it was one of the baptismal
formularies, such as we have in the Apostles'
Creed, modified by phrases imported from the
Nicene Faith. Some scholars hold that it received its exact form and was officially adopted
by the second ecumenical council at Constantinople in 381, and for that reason should be
called Constantinopolitan rather than Nicene;
but owing to the faulty records of this assembly,
we have no assurance of such a procedure. Our
first precise information is that the Council of
Chalcedon, which confirmed the Nicene Faith,
also accepted the creed, together with the Tome
of Leo and other documents, as orthodox in
their content. Hence perhaps arose the confusion in the popular mind between the Nicene
Faith and the Nicene Creed as equivalent for-
mulae. But the creed was not introduced into
the liturgical service of the eastern Church
earlier than 565, under the Emperor Julian II.
In the West it seems to have been employed
liturgically first among the Spaniards. The

notorious phrase *filioque,* which makes the
Holy Ghost proceed "from the Son" as well as
from the Father, was added in that country,
and, though favoured by Charlemagne, did not
receive the final sanction of Rome until the
year 1014.

The important point in all this is, not that the
bishops in their proceedings at Chalcedon admitted the Nicene Creed as orthodox, but that
the Definition then promulgated, the act for
which the council stands in history, is based on
the Nicene Faith alone and in itself takes no
account of any of the creeds. And the significance of this exclusion lies in the fact that—
with the exception of a bare mention of the
Holy Ghost, who is not definitely personified—
the whole content of the Profession, as the
Faith and the Definition together may be
named, is concerned with the Incarnation and
its immediate implications. Belief in God the
Creator and Father, in the office of Christ as
Saviour and Judge, and in his resurrection as
essential to that office, is necessarily included.
Belief also in the virgin birth is inculcated, but
only in the Definition, not in the original Faith,
and there evidently as a somewhat reluctant
concession to the Alexandrian mania for the

Theotokos. As for the articles of belief which appear in the creed alone, as I have said before, it is not to be supposed that they were omitted from the Profession because there was any doubt in regard to them. Whatever may be the date and origin of the Nicene Creed, every clause embraced in it—the personification of the Holy Ghost, the Catholic Church, baptism for the remission of sins, the resurrection of the body, the future life—all of these were fully accepted at the time of Chalcedon, as indeed they had been at the time of Nicea, so generally accepted that no serious discussion had arisen over them. They were passed over in the Profession because, by a kind of prophetic instinct, the Greek Fathers felt them to be subordinate to the virgin birth and resurrection of Christ, and still lower in importance than the cardinal fact of the Word made flesh about which all the major heresies had raged. And I think that no more vital task confronts the Church today than to recognize the urgent necessity of insisting on the unreserved acceptance of the one dogma of the Incarnation as the definite, clear, and common mark of a Christian, while leaving to the conscience of each individual how far he will interpret the accessory articles of faith as literal or symbolical, as fact or poetry. Such a distinction would not mean that the Nicene Creed should be withdrawn from the liturgy; on the contrary it would enable many a devout soul to join in pronouncing the creed, who now hesitates or refrains because he feels that some of the clauses, though profoundly significant for the religious life if taken symbolically, cannot be held in quite the literal sense intended by their framers. It is to distinguish between what is essential and permanent and immutable, and that which must change with the changing modes of thought.

CHAPTER X

THE DOCTRINE OF THE LOGOS

Our hasty survey of the literature from the fourth Gospel to the Council of Chalcedon has been directed to bring out this one fact, that the Greek Fathers of the age were concerned with the dogma of the Incarnation as the all-important basis of Christianity, so important that beside it every other question sinks into comparative insignificance. It might seem that religion was narrowed and impoverished by this focusing of attention upon a single point, but I think such a view will not be advocated by anyone who considers all that is involved in this article of faith, or who knows how thoroughly this same problem has again absorbed the minds of theologians during the past century. It is not a little thing to believe that Jesus of Nazareth was the Son of God as well as the Son of man. And when this myth, in itself the amazing consummation of Hebrew prophecy, comes to us interpreted through the Hellenic philosophy of the logos, surely anyone may be satisfied with the richness of its content. And so I propose, in these remaining pages, to show what this dogma meant to the ancient Church and, incidentally, what it may mean to us.

At the outset we are met by a difficulty. How shall we translate the term *logos* and its derivative *logikos*? For the first we have grown accustomed to "word," following the Latin usage of *verbum* (though the Tertullian *sermo* was perhaps a nearer translation); and this would be fairly adequate if we could always remember that the original for which it stands meant, as its Latin and English substitutes in themselves do not mean, both an unexpressed thought within the mind and a thought expressed in words. It denotes, that is, in the most general way what is mental or spiritual as distinguished from what is physical or material, and so is often synonymous with "wisdom" or the Platonic "Idea" or, as we shall see, "purpose"; it signifies both the "large discourse of reason, looking before and after," and the means by which mind or spirit declares itself in operation or communicates with other minds and spirits. On the whole it will be better, and

will cause no embarrassment, to employ the
term *logos* itself as if it were Anglicized, as
indeed it almost is. But for the derivative *logikos* we have no such ease. Neither "verbal" nor
"spiritual" is a tolerable translation, while
"logical" has become so restricted in meaning
as to have lost all its religious value. In this
dilemma the lesser of two evils is to fall back on
the literal transcript, despite its awkwardness
and its liability to misunderstanding. I must
ask the reader to forget the connexion of "logical" with formal logic as a technique of syl-
logistic reasoning, and to take the adjective as
signifying simply "that which is related to
logos" or, more specifically, "that which consciously possesses logos." Such indeed was the
common usage among theologians.

Now to these ancient theologians, trained in
the tradition of Hebrew prophecy and in the
language of the Academy and the Porch, the
whole extent of the universe was permeated
with logos. Looking upon the populous tribes
of plants and animals, impressed, as Aristotle
had been in an earlier age, by the curious ad-
justment of part to part in their structure and
by the mutual adaptation between them and
their environment, moved above all by the

mystery of their beauty which seems to tran-
scend any conscious or unconscious need in
their own existence, the Fathers could explain
such phenomena only as the work of a shaping
and governing intelligence. To this creative
logos they attributed the miraculous growth of
a plant from the seed; from this they derived
the cunning provision of nature by which the
hare and other defenceless animals were pro-
lific, whereas the lioness, as they thought, bore
only one cub at long intervals. Only so could
they understand the wisdom of the birds, which
brought these aerial passengers to and fro over
the wide expanses of sea and land, the providence that teaches the ants to lay up their win-
ter store, and many another activity of the
lesser creatures for which science could offer no
satisfactory account. Christ, they believed, was
alluding to the mystery of the logos when he
bade his disciples to consider the lilies of the
field, which of themselves could take no thought
yet were arrayed in beauty beyond even the
glory of Solomon. Above all, these theologians,
like the philosophers before them and, we may
add, like many a poet since, were filled with awe
by the greater spectacle of inanimate nature,—
the majestic revolution of the stars, the recur-

rent swell of the tides beneath the moon, and the restraining of the vexed waters of the sea within their bounds. These things, they argued, do not happen by chance or by some blind law of corporeal matter. All this that we see, exclaims an unknown writer, is a manifestation of the "holy and incomprehensible logos."[1]

But if the phenomenal world, including plants and animals, is a manifestation of some controlling logos, it is still not logical in the sense that it consciously possesses logos; for that gift we must look elsewhere. "What a piece of work is man! how noble in reason!" Hamlet exclaims; "how infinite in faculty!" Now that *noble in reason* is precisely what the Greek theologians meant by distinguishing man from other creatures as alone logical. By virtue of that faculty he, and he only, enters into the life of animals and comprehends the actions which they perform under the impulse of a reason not consciously their own. He weighs the stars and measures their orbits; to him the light of the setting sun and the birth of morning become instinct with the joys of

[1] *Ep. ad Diogn.*, vii.—The preceding sentences and many that follow in this and the next chapter are a cento from Athanasius and other Greek theologians. To give the references for all such passages would clutter up these pages intolerably.

beauty; so that the heavens are unrolled before his eyes like a celestial book. While the body sleeps, something of his mind goes forth to wander in distant places and creates for him marvellous adventures. And what else is all this but the work of a "logical soul," which enables him to behold the invisible reasons that lie behind the forms and motions of things visible?

And man is logical not only by possession of the faculty of thought and comprehension and by the gift of silent discourse within his own mind, but he is endowed also with the faculty of language, by which he embodies his ideas in symbolic sounds and signs and sends them forth to live a kind of life of their own.[2] Thus it is that logos communes with logos, and a man knows himself to be not solitary in a friendless world, but member of a great society of kindred souls.

So far the philosophy of the Church is scarcely distinguishable from that of the Porch. The divergence begins, and grows as wide as the removal of the heavens from the earth, when this doctrine is made the basis of religion. It was inevitable that the Stoic, from his conception of a conscious logos in the highest divi-

2 The λόγος προφορικός.

sion of nature, should think of the power which
governs the whole of nature as possessing the
same consciousness; and what is such a power
but God? There are in fact passages, and many
of them, in Cleanthes and Epictetus and the
Roman Stoics wherein the cosmic logos is endowed with all the characteristics of a deity
worthy of homage and love; but if the disciples
of Zeno sometimes worshipped, it was yet at
the price of sacrificing their principles. So far
as the logos could be regarded by them consistently as God, it was a divinity within and
of the world, the "spirit within" and the "in-
exorable fate" of Virgil, and their religious
emotion properly assumed that pantheistic
tinge which has coloured so much of the natu-
ralism of later ages:

> A presence that disturbs me with the joy
> Of elevated thoughts; a sense sublime
> Of something far more deeply interfused,
> Whose dwelling is the light of setting suns,
> And the round ocean and the living air,
> And the blue sky, and in the mind of man.

I would not deny the exquisite charm of such
a feeling towards nature; nevertheless, even at
its best and purest, pantheism is a kind of half-
way house, and no abiding place for the spirit
of man. He who stops there will find himself

after a while turned out upon the common high-
way, obliged to journey forwards to belief in
a frankly personal deity, or backwards to an
avowed atheism.[3] And so we meet with a curious lack of equilibrium in these ancient panthe-
ists of the Porch. At times they beheld God and
worshipped; but the backward direction was
ever the easier and more consistent course for
them. The legitimate goal of Stoicism, as indeed its real starting point, was the scientific
conception of the universe as a product of unconscious, unpurposing, mechanistic energy,
for which the feeling of reverence is a meaningless sentimentality; its native mood, as we see
it in Marcus Aurelius, is rather resignation
towards things as they are than adoration of a
Being beyond these tides of mortal change.

Now to the Christian, for all he borrowed
from the Stoic philosophy, the ultimate merging together of spirit and matter seemed to
savour of the Arian blasphemies which had
lowered the logos to be an integral part of
creation.[4] Save in his most unguarded hours he

---

[3] The former, for example, was the path taken by Wordsworth,
as may be seen by comparing the *Tintern Abbey* from which I
have quoted with the religious note of his later poems. Lucretius
virtually went the other way.

[4] So Athanasius, *Contra Ar.*, ii, 11.

was never a pantheist; God for him was always a Creator living outside of that which He created, immanent by His power, but essentially transcendent; the logos in the world was merely the image, or effluence, of a higher Logos identical with the wisdom and will of a supermundane Person.

To us of today, perhaps, with our larger knowledge of the complex construction of the universe and our theory of evolution, the chief interest in the logos will be its connexion with the idea of purpose, or teleology. Now the teleological view of existence was not unknown to the pagan philosophers, and in particular it plays a dominant rôle in the system of Aristotle. But the Peripatetic conception of *telos,* though in ethics it made purpose the guiding principle of conduct, quite definitely excluded the notion of cosmic purpose, and that in two ways. In the first place Aristotle looked upon the universe as without beginning or conclusion, as uncreated and eternally the same. In this scheme there is no progress from grade to grade in time, from species to species, but a coexistent scale of species showing a kind of geometric pattern. Each species is a finished unit, having its own end, while within the species each individual

has a *telos* in itself, a potential perfection of its
own nature, to which it may or may not actually attain. And in the second place, though
Aristotle might seem to have raised teleology
to its highest point by his conception of God as
the absolute final cause, as the object, that is,
of all desire and thus the source of all motion
in the moving worlds, yet in reality he rendered
the idea jejune by depriving this first cause of
any reciprocal participation in the transactions
of time. His God, so far from being personal,
is not even an efficient cause, but a pure abstraction lifted out of all contact with things as
they are. Aristotle perceived design in the
world, but did not infer from this an interested
designer; in other words his cosmic *telos* is in
no proper sense a purpose, an end proposed by
an agent who adopts means to its fulfilment,
though without such an implication it is hard to
see just what force is left to the term. A static
impersonal teleology must be set down as one
of the grandiose confusions of human thought.

Beat about as we will, there are only two conclusions in which the philosophic mind can
abide. Either, as the Hindu in his more coura-
geous moods taught, the whole thing, this globe
and this life, are utterly without design, a phan-

tasmagoria in which we can detect no meaning
and to which we have no right to apply any
interpretation, not even that of chance, a huge
illusion of ignorance which simply vanishes into
nothing at the touch of knowledge; or else, if
we see design in the world, then there is no
holding back from the inference of the theist.
The agnostic will say that this is to fall into
anthropomorphism. It is. But design itself is
already an anthropomorphic term; and to admit the existence of design while refusing to see
that it implies purpose, and to admit the existence of purpose while refusing to acknowledge a purposing mind, is the folly of half-
heartedness. On the other hand the agnostic
who, denying plan and purpose, thinks he can
stop short of the philosophy of pure illusion,
resembles a man who boasts that he can walk on
water.

It is here that Christianity brought consistency to the teleology of the schools by going
behind the logos of the Stoic and behind the
Aristotelian *telos* to Plato's intuition of a divine Providence, which is further vitalized and
enriched by grafting it upon the lore of the Hebrew prophets and the faith of the gospel. For
the logos of theology was not only the manifes-

tation of design in the world, but the wisdom of foresight (*pronoia*), a divine *purpose* realizing itself through the ages in the economy of creation and salvation, "the manifold wisdom of God, according to the eternal purpose (*prothesis*) which He purposed in Christ Jesus." It is true, of course, that the Fathers had no more notion than did their pagan contemporaries of development in the scientific sense of the word; but it is true also that the *logos-pronoia-prothesis* of Christianity can be adapted perfectly to our modern views, is in fact a very natural complement of any tenable theory of evolution.

The comely order of the world, that which we mean by calling it a cosmos, was, then, to the Christian a reflection of the logos as creative purpose; while in the soul of man the logos answers to logos not as an inert reflection, but as a conscious participation. Thus to Basil, looking upon nature under the glorifying rays of the sun, it seemed as though he could hear the ancient word of commendation, "God saw the light that it was good"; and to Clement it seemed that he could behold the Lord "resting in joy upon the work of His hands."

But there was another side to the picture. This cosmos, stamped and sealed as it is with the divine signature, is yet subject to strange imperfections and marks of error,—calamities of the heavens, floods and disasters upon the earth, among living creatures the cruelty of life that depends on the death of other lives. And consider the state of man. We appear to be made for knowledge and admiration; yet how often our heritage of happiness is exchanged for cloying pleasures, and our aspiring desires into ugly lusts with their uglier consequences—sickness, envy, madness, and all their train. Read the pages of history, and it will appear almost that the divine logos has been not so much thwarted by man as turned into a diabolical ingenuity of evil. Hence the question that has troubled the minds of all philosophers and all theologians, the insistent distracting query: *Unde malum?*

By the Greek philosophers generally evil was defined as a form of ignorance, with the Socratic corollary that knowledge and virtue are identical. That is to say: taking evil to be by definition that which results in discomfiture and misery, they held that no man will knowingly choose his own perdition. Theoretically such a view would seem to be sound, but in practice, as Aristotle showed, it fails to explain our conduct. How shall we reconcile it with the common fact of experience, which Ovid has expressed in the familiar epigram: "I see and approve the better, I follow the worse"?

Christian theologians, on the other hand, however they wrangled in other matters, agreed almost without exception in stressing the human (or the Satanic) will as the prime factor in evil. With their theory of creation they were bound to regard existence in itself as essentially good, and to define evil as a negation of existence, or, so far as it could be called positive, as an uncaused revolt of the created will against God's will. "Man," says Methodius, speaking for the orthodox Church, "was created with free will, not as if anything already evil pre-existed which it lay in the power of man to choose if he wished, . . . but the act of obedience or of disobedience to God is the only cause. That is the very meaning of free will."[5] Now this association of evil with the will certainly touches a profound psychological truth; and it has this great advantage, that it accords with our sense of responsibility for wrongdoing which is one of the ultimate facts of human consciousness, and which the Greeks, including

[5] *De Libero Arbitrio*, 265 (Migne).

Plato, fully recognized but found difficult to reconcile with their equation of vice with ignorance. We consider the inanimate world, and the interruptions of order may perhaps have the appearance of inevitable law, as though they were necessary parts of a larger design; or we regard the miseries of human life about us, and again we may seem to discern the operation of an ineluctable fatality, as though men were the puppets of inheritance and circumstance. But we look then into ourselves, and the more honest and penetrating our gaze, the more deeply are we convinced, despite all the apologetic devices of reason, that to our own undoing we have deliberately chosen the perverse ways of wrong, that the disease is inherent in our very heart and will. The responsibility for evil, the Christian says, as Plato had said before him, lies with man, not with God. All this is well and plausible, yet something still is omitted. The innate sense of responsibility may point to the will as the errant faculty, but the question persists: how can we hold a man, how can we hold ourselves, accountable unless, when the will makes its decision, it does so with full knowledge of the consequences of our acts? In some way both the will and the intelligence must be concerned together in our definition of right and wrong.

So judged, I am inclined to admire the Athanasian theory of evil as that which, of all theories before or after, draws most deeply from the wells of human experience, and as the most thoroughly Christian.[6]

According to this theory the world, as the evocation of the divine logos, was originally without blemish, fashioned to be the fit and perfect home of creatures composed of soul and body. And the souls of men, for whom this dwelling was prepared, were created in the likeness of God, and as such possessed the special faculty of seeing and knowing their Maker; they were designed to be members of the great society of holy beings, angels and archangels, whose life consists in the joyous contemplation of spiritual things.[7] All this is implied by calling man "logical." But the principle of mutability is inherent in the very nature of all created things alike, only with this difference that to man was given the capacity of free

---

[6] The following exposition of the Athanasian theory of evil is based on the opening section of the *Contra Gentes.*

[7] Συνδιαιτᾶσθαι τοῖς ἁγίοις ἐν τῇ τῶν νοητῶν θεωρίᾳ. These "spiritual things," *noêta,* are the Platonic Ideas. It is noteworthy that Athanasius does not merge them into the being of God.

will and self-determination which was withheld
from inanimate objects and illogical animals.
In this union of free will and mutability lies the
honour of man, but also his peculiar peril of
responsibility. His true motion, that for which
he was designed, should be ever upwards to his
Creator and towards a clearer vision of the
fair realities of the spirit (*ta onta kai kala*);
there is his goal, and in that direction he acquires the unity and uniformity and happiness
and safety which he craves.[8] But this motion of
the soul towards what is akin to its nature but
ever beyond its perfect comprehension, requires
a continuity of attention and energy not easy
for a creature of whose very essence mutability
is a constituent; there is needed a constant effort of the will, while this effort of the will is
conditioned by a clear intuition of the object
to be attained. Hence arise the hesitation and
reluctance of the soul, its fitful purpose, and
its turning away to the less exacting contemplation of itself and its own activities in the
body. The beginning of evil for Athanasius was
thus a kind of *rhathymia,* that slackness of attention or failure of energy, at once the cause
and the effect of ignorance, which hinders the

8 Compare the importance of the single σκοπός in *Laws,* xii.

soul, as St. Paul lamented, from pressing on to "the mark for the prize of the high calling of God."[9]

This was the Fall, when, caught by the delusion of forbidden power that appeared to lie within their grasp, men fell into desire of themselves, humouring their own way above the contemplation of things divine. It was as if man, by shutting the eyes of the spirit, created about himself an artificial darkness, wherein these bodies and the dull objects of our touch seem alone to be visible (*blepomena*), while the realities of the spiritual life fade into invisibility. That which was intended to be an instrument is converted into an end, and all the orders of being are thrown into disarray. The whole scale of values is inverted; pleasure assumes an importance not properly belonging to it; new desires spring up with new objects of desire, which in their fulfilment produce greed, injustice, theft, adultery, murder, and all the train of criminal aberrations. By the defalca-

---

[9] For *rhathymia* as a cause of evil implicit also in Greek intellectualism, see *The Religion of Plato,* chap. ix. Cf. *Sophist* 254A: τὰ γὰρ τῆς τῶν πολλῶν ὄμματα καρτερεῖν πρὸς τὸ θεῖον ἀφορῶντα ἀδύνατα. This also, removed from the sphere of theology, is Aristotle's notion of δύναμις and ἐνέργεια reaching their ἐντελέχεια in pure θεωρία. And Plotinus, among his other views, held that evil begins for the soul when it turns from the contemplation of Being to consideration of its own state of Becoming (I, viii, 4).

tion of man the world is altered into something which had no place in the original design of the Creator. In the widest sense of the word this state of mind is idolatry, which, taking its start from sluggishness of will, ends in worship of mere idols of the imagination instead of the eternal realities.[10] "He (the Logos) was in the world, and the world was made by him, and the world knew him not"; in the self-engendered night of evil man has ceased to be logical.

Such is the Athanasian account of evil. And on the whole I doubt if philosophy, or psychology if you prefer the word, has ever shown a profounder insight into the actual working of the human soul. For, when stripped of its mythological trappings, it is just this infirmity of *rhathymia* that drags us down from spiritual peace and unity to the tragical conflict of the pleasures of the senses; it is this compound of sloth and ignorance that creates the slough of sin into which the life of man has fallen. So far analysis of the actual experience of life may

[10] It is not fantastic to compare this reduction of all evil to a form of idolatry with the *eidôlopoiïa* which Plato, in the *Sophist,* held to be the characteristic activity and the initial error of those who sought for reality in the shadows of appearance instead of in the eternal Ideas. When he declares that sophistry is the "primary falsehood" in the heart, he is merely saying in other language what Christ meant by calling Satan "a liar and the father of lies."

carry us into the *what* of evil. But the theory of
Athanasius, it will be observed, is not metaphysical: it does not explain *why* this defection
of will should trouble the energy of a creature
endowed with free power of choice and having
his natural good displayed before him; it leaves
the ultimate *whence* of evil a mystery involved
in the very act of creation, still unreconciled
with any conception of an absolute cause. And
in this it agrees, better perhaps than its ex-
pounder knew, with the dualism of Plato's
Timaeus, which simply posits evil as a final inexplicable Necessity in the nature of things.

CHAPTER XI

THE LOGOS (*continued*)

THE Athanasian theory of the fall of man, whether it be taken as history or allegory, accords well with the actual condition of the world: on the one side a God whose logos has gone out in a vast work of creation, on the other side the most highly endowed creature, the conscious percipient of the divine purpose, falling away to worship of idols of his own imagination. As Athanasius says, "man, the logical, created in the image of deity, was disappearing, and the handiwork of God was in process of dissolution."[1] Certainly He who wrought the design would not suffer it to perish, nor permit His purpose to be utterly frustrated, though it might be temporarily marred and hindered. And certainly "it will appear not inconsonant that the Father should effect salvation of the world by means of that through

---

[1] *De Incarnatione*, vi, 1.

which He created it."[2] The logos was the instrument of creation, it should be the instrument of restoration: that is the sum of the Christian scheme of Soteriology. Now the mere notion that the salvation of man comes through the logos is not new; it animates the Idealism of Plato, though the word commonly employed by him is *nous,* reason, and it gives force to the dogma of the Stoics. But by association with the Messianic belief of Israel something is added to the philosophy of the logos which Greece had never known.

In the synoptic Gospels Jesus is regarded as the Son of God, and this belief is carried on and deepened in the body of the fourth Gospel. But also in the prologue to the fourth Gospel the idea is thrown out that the Saviour of the world is the creative logos of God. Implicitly then, though the statement is not made explicitly, the Son of God and the Logos of God are one and the same: the Son as the Logos is identified with the creative wisdom and purpose of deity, the Logos as the Son is hypostatized into a person beside the person of the Father. At one bound the philosophy of the logos has become a religion. And there is a striking corollary to

[2] *Ibid.,* i, 4.

this thesis: the Logos hypostatized as the only begotten Son bears a different relation to God the Father from that borne to God the Creator by the logos within man. We too as possessors of the word may be called after a fashion children of the Most High and sons of the Father, but as creatures of His will we are not of His substance and nature, however we may be like Him; and on this difference depends the possibility of our present state of disgrace. The distinction was made in Origen metaphysically by calling the Logos the eternally begotten Son, whereas the birth of man is an event in time. Athanasius expresses the same idea scripturally by a quaint interpretation of the words of Genesis: "Let us make man in our image, after our likeness." The Father, he says, is here speaking to the Son (hence the "us"); the Logos-Son is the image, whereas man is created in the likeness of the image, to possess as it were "certain shadows of the Logos and so to be not the Logos but logical."[3] It follows also

---

[3] *Ibid.*, iii, 3. The logos of man differs from the πρωτότυπον in being τρεπτός, subject to mutation. This is not to say that the divine Logos, as ἄτρεπτος, is fixed in stark immutability, but that through all its changes its essential nature remains unaffected. In man change is of the radical sort designated by the Stoics as "passion," πάθος. See *De Inc.*, iii, 4; Gregory Nyssen, *De Hominis Op.*, 184c (Migne), and *In Verba Faciamus Hominem*, 264A, c (Migne).

that when we speak of the human logos we do not think of this as an hypostasis distinct from the hypostasis of the man himself, but as the characteristic quality of man as man.

The drama of redemption then will be the interaction between the Logos-Son of God and the logical nature of man, whereby the effects of sin will be cancelled and man shall be restored to the likeness of the image in which he was fashioned. In that drama the great event, the *peripeteia* so to speak, is to the Christian the Incarnation; but this is by no means an isolated incident or unrelated to the general course of history. Rather, as Justin declared in the passage quoted at the beginning of our study,[4] all the wisdom of the philosophers, all the precepts of the lawgivers and the example of the sages, had been a response in the heart of man to the manifestation of the logos in the world. Justin might have added that literature and art, so long as they remain true to their high function and do not sink into mere flattery of man's baser instincts, are an effort to interpret life and the phenomena of nature in the light of the logos, and to build here and now a home for the soul in the world of Ideas. And

[4] See *ante,* p. 9.

for the scholar the finest and most comprehensive name ever yet devised is the old Greek term *logios,* signifying one who is skilled to trace the operations of the logos, to distinguish its genuine expression in literature from shams, to know the truth, and so to dwell in the calm yet active leisure (*scholê*) of contemplation. The scholar, the *logios,* in that noble sense of the word, is he who by study and reflection has recovered the birthright of humanity and holds it in fee for the generations to come.

But in our darkened state the drag of the flesh is heavy, the seductions of the world are insidious,[5] the weight of sin, as the Christian would say, overwhelming, so that, left to itself, the spirit of man might seem bound to sit for ever in a closed prison with only narrow and fleeting glimpses of the larger light. Hence there was needed a more direct illumination than is afforded by the logical order of nature and life, and to the Christian the special work of redemption began with the self-revelation of God to Israel through the inspired lawgivers and prophets. I fancy that to the reader of today—though it would not have been so a few

---

[5] This is the famous πιθανότης τῶν πραγμάτων of the Stoics. See *Hellenistic Philosophies,* 151.

years since—the most surprising feature of
patristic literature is the constant and systematic conversion of the Old Testament into an
allegory of the Logos. This reinterpretation of
Scripture was begun for the Jews themselves
—so far as the records are extant—by Philo; it
was turned to the service of the new faith by the
earliest Christian writers and developed with
all the extravagance of an uncritical imagination, particularly by Origen who raised the allegorical method of exegesis into an erudite
bibliolatry. Whenever the voice of God is heard
or the angel of the Lord appears, it was taken
to be a direct revelation, not of the Father, but
of the Logos-Son; types of Christ were discovered in the most unexpected places, all prophecy centred upon the coming event of the Incarnation, and every word, each syllable, was
probed for hidden treasure. It need not be said
that much of this interpretation is from one
point of view without critical or historical basis;
yet one may well doubt whether our present
habit of rejecting the whole method and of
minimizing the prophetic element of the Old
Testament is not equally erroneous in the other
direction. Many of the passages supposed by
ancient theology to refer to the coming Messiah

may have had quite a different and more literal
meaning to the contemporary Jews; but to
read Scripture without perceiving that an undefined Messianic hope was an inheritance of
the Hebrew race throughout the ages, that in
their subconscious mind, as we might say, the
notion of a divine deliverer lay always dormant,
ready at any moment to flash out into clear expression, that the whole course of Israelitic
history unrolls as a kind of mystical progress
towards one grand event, to overlook the fact
that the New Testament is a close continuation
of the Old and a consummation of what had
been long preparing, not to see that the Johannine Logos is the secular realization of the un-
quenchable Messianic hopes and can be read
back legitimately into the ancient theology of
Israel as, so to speak, its implicit *telos*,—this, I
say, is the greater failure in scholarship and a
more unpardonæble dereliction of intelligence.
Bibliolatry has slain its thousands, but biblio-
phoby may slay its tens of thousands; for it is
still true that the letter killeth.

Thus from one point of view the Incarnation
may be regarded as the closing event, in the
fulness of time, of a long series of transactions,
while from another point of view it is unique in

character. Hitherto the Logos might be known
as a creative and providential and admonitive
force, manifesting itself indeed to those who
could read the signs, but always as a director
behind the scenes; now, at the climax of the
drama, it comes forth upon the stage and takes
its part openly among the actors, a veritable
deus ex machina. The meaning and purpose of
this theophany were concentrated by Irenaeus
into a brief formula, which the Church never
forgot, and about which Athanasius in particular wove the fabric of his *De Incarnatione* as
a tremendous fugue upon a single theme: "God
became man in order that man might become
God."[6] The divine Logos, that is to say, condescended to the conditions of human life, in
order that the logos of man might be raised to
its prerogative as conscious bearer of the likeness of God. In that act of re-creation the
Greek theologians by analysis discovered four
leading moments: (1) revelation, (2) imitation, (3) grace, (4) vicarious atonement.

I. Obviously the epiphany of the Logos is

[6] So it is the fashion to translate the formula as given, *e.g. De
Inc.*, liv, 3: αὐτὸς γὰρ ἐνηνθρώπησεν ἵνα ἡμεῖς θεοποιηθῶμεν. A more
exact version would be: "For he himself put on human nature
(or, came to live among men) in order that we might be made
like to God." The *theos* of the compound is a word characteristically Greek in its fluidity, and may mean "god," or "a god," or

first of all and through all an act of revelation.
The consequence of the Fall, as a declension of
the soul from allegiance to the Creator to concern with the creature was, in a word, idolatry.
To the early converts this idolatry appeared
primarily as the worship of images and of the
innumerable gods who were themselves creatures fallen from grace, if not mere phantoms
of human conceit; but the most stubborn foe of
the Christian, as it had been of the Platonic,
faith was that homage to the idols of the reason
which wears the mask of philosophy. Call it
Stoicism or call it Epicureanism, call it science
or deism or realism or mere indifference or
what you will, the most insidious and obstinate
enemy of religion was, and is, the subservience
of the mind content to see in the world only a
huge fatalistic mechanism or a heterogeneous
product of chance or, as the modern Darwin-
ians would have it, a monstrous combination of
both. Whatever form the error may take, it is a
denial of the Logos as the creative wisdom and
purpose of God, a magnification of the creature, a refined, but none the less devastating
species of idolatry. Against this defection to

a "godlike being." Here the third sense is evidently intended,
and there is nothing in the orthodox use of the formula to warrant the sort of mysticism implied in the meaning "god."

idols, whether of the imagination or of the reason, God had protested by the majesty of His
works and more directly through the mouth of
inspired sage and prophet appealing to the
silent witness within the breast of every man.
There was needed a more definite and immediate manifestation of the truth, and this to
the Christian was given when the Word became
flesh.

The Word became flesh: it is a portentous
saying, not easy for men of our day to accept in
its simplicity, nor did it make its way in the ancient world without contradiction and ridicule;
to the Greek it appeared at first as foolishness
and to the Jew a stumbling block. I would not
slur over these difficulties, but there are certain
considerations, not unknown to the Greek apologists, that may mitigate the objections of reason. In the first place if there be a God, is it
not reasonable that He should reveal Himself?
Is it not the case that, so far as we are concerned, an unrevealed God is the same as no
God? that an unrevealed God might as well not
exist, properly speaking does not exist, for
us? The Great Unknowable does not offer a
subject very fruitful for contemplation or very
serviceable for the wants of mankind. And,

secondly, if God was to reveal Himself, how
could this be done effectively save through
some such act as the Incarnation? How should
the poison of idolatry be counteracted save by
some miraculous intervention manifesting the
existence of a divine purpose in the world yet
not of the world? How can we conceive purpose
save as the will and intelligence of a person directed to the accomplishment of some end?
How could man be made to grasp the reality
of a person except under such conditions as sur-
round and limit his own being? How otherwise
could such conditions be assumed than through
the visible embodiment of the Logos as an
historical event in time and place?

All this is conveyed in the saying: The Word
became flesh. But it is important to add that
the Greek theologians, though they held the
appearance of the Logos in human form to be a
true revelation of God, were emphatic in de-
claring it to be not a *complete* revelation of God.
Over and over again they are careful to assert
that the expression Father and Son applied to
two persons of the Godhead, while true so far
as it goes, is only the translation into human
language of a mystery which transcends the

human understanding, and that the exhibition of the divine attributes in the life and death of the incarnate Logos did not exhaust the fulness of the divine essence. This reverent reservation was the excuse, if any there be, for their employment of such terms as infinite and omnipotent and omnipresent and the like abstractions in their definition of that which might better have been left undefined; it was a not wholly fortunate way of avowing that what we know of God by revelation is the truth but only a little of the truth.

II. The purpose of the special manifestation of divine purpose, if the play on words be permitted, was that man, made in the image of God and logical, but fallen into illogical idolatry, might be restored to his high estate, and that so the frustrated plan of creation might be fulfilled; or as some would say, preferring the language of Aristotle to that of mythology, that man in the course of time might attain in actuality to the potential perfection of his nature. So God, at the opportune moment, revealed Himself in order that man might recover, or reach, the divine likeness by imitating what he beheld.

Now this doctrine of imitation, as I have said

elsewhere,[7] was not discovered or invented by
those of the new faith. It lies at the very core of
Plato's theology and so of the Greek tradition;
and it has never been expressed more clearly
than in the great passage of the *Theaetetus,* of
which echoes can be heard in endless variations
through the literature, pagan and Christian, of
the following ages:

"But it is not possible that evils should cease
to be—since by reason of necessity there exists
always something contrary to the good—
neither can they have their seat among the gods,
but of necessity they haunt mortal nature and
this region of ours. Wherefore our aim should
be to escape hence to that other world with all
speed. And the way of escape is by becoming
like to God in so far as we may. And the becoming like is in becoming just and holy
by taking thought. . . . God is never in any
wise unjust, but most perfectly just, and there
is nothing more like to Him than one of us who
should make himself just to the limit of man's
power."

At first thought on reading these words, one
may ask what Christianity has to offer that is
not here; but second thought makes one aware
of a subtle difference. And then if, with this

7 See *The Religion of Plato,* 37ff.

passage in mind, one turns to the sermons of
Gregory Nyssen on the Lord's Prayer and the
Beatitudes,[8] in which the Platonic doctrine of
homoiôsis, or imitation, is developed into a marvellous treatise on the Christian life, one sees
how profoundly the sentiment has been transformed by its reference to the Incarnation. The
change might be expressed, though inade-
quately of course, in epigrammatic form by
saying that in Platonism man imitates God by
becoming just and holy, whereas in Christianity man becomes just and holy by imitating
God. With Plato, even when his philosophy
slants most strongly towards religion, the ethical Ideas are the outstanding reality, the fixed
point of belief, while God, for all that we hear
of creation and providence, remains still a somewhat shadowy figure, now appearing and now
fading into the background. It is precisely
otherwise with the Christian. To him the ethical
Ideas owe their cogency to the fact that they are
personified in the Logos, and we are able to
make them our own by imitating the Logos as
revealed in a life passed under human con-

[8] I should reckon these sermons *De Oratione Dominica* and *De
Beatitudinibus* together about the finest treatise on Christian
ethics known to me. They ought to be made available in separate
publication, properly edited with text, translation, and notes.

ditions. "No one but His own Word," says
Irenaeus, "could tell us the things of the
Father. . . . And we could not apprehend
them otherwise than by seeing our Master and
hearing his voice, in order that by imitating his
actions and fulfilling his words we might be
brought into communion with him."[9]

It is properly the human aspect of the Master's life that draws us first as we read the
gospel narrative, his unblemished purity and
strong humility and his love for God and man.[10]
The clear beauty of his character acts as an
almost irresistible incentive to imitation, or at
least to the desire of imitation; while his perfect
humanity is like a voice saying in our ears:
Thou too canst live today as he once lived, and
so win for thyself such purity and humility and
love. And then, perhaps, something in the story,
those surprising sentences that had no place on
merely mortal lips, the signals of a miraculous
power and authority held in check,—something
warns us that here is man yet also more than
man. We remember the prologue to his life in
the fourth Gospel: "In the beginning was the

[9] *Contra Haer.*, V, i, 1.
[10] The place of these three virtues in the teaching of the Gospels
I have discussed in *The Christ of the New Testament*, chaps.
v and vi.

Word, and the Word was with God, and the
Word was God. . . . And the Word was made
flesh, and dwelt among us." And so remember-
ing, if we are capable of rising to the high theology of the Logos, we discover a new meaning
in these virtues set before us as models, a meaning so sublime that, as Gregory says, the very
thought thereof affects us with a dizziness like
that which comes upon one who from the edge
of a lofty promontory looks down upon the remote floor of the sea. He who, imitating the
purity of Jesus, purges himself of the clinging
passions of the world, will discern in his own
heart, as in a burnished mirror, a living image
of the transcendent holiness of the Father. If
he imitates the humility of Jesus, he will then
know that he has set himself to follow after one
who, though he thought it not robbery to be the
equal of God, yet humbled himself to the endurance of human infirmities and to the Cross.
And beyond this purity and this humility lies
the sublime charity moving within the circle of
the divine nature and reaching therefrom out
towards creation, of which mystery we get a
glimpse in the saying: "God so loved the world
that he gave his only begotten Son." Does the
Great Commandment imply that here, in the

highest reach of imitation, we should be included in this love not by passive reception only but by active participation?

That and something more than that. In the fifth of his sermons on the Lord's Prayer, when he comes to the clause on the forgiveness of trespasses, Gregory, trembling for his own audacity, ventures to hint at a strange inversion of what might seem to be the natural order of things. Our duty and our hope of happiness, as he has shown, depend on making ourselves like to God; but here on the contrary we are bidden to ask that God should become like to us, that He should forgive *as and if we forgive*. In pointing to this reciprocity in the law of imitation, Gregory touches on an amazing enigma of the economy, which yet, as we see if we stop to reflect, is based on necessity. For any true similarity must be mutual, and A cannot resemble B unless at the same time B resembles A. And so, with a slight change in the language of the famous maxim, we may say indeed that God imitated (*i.e.* became) man in order that man might imitate God; but we may add in our thoughts that without the second clause the first would be void and meaningless. We may even go further and assert that the moral response of human nature is the cause and inevitable condition of the divine condescension, as though God could not have loved Himself and the world were there not potentially in the heart of man a similar love of his fellows and of God.

By such steps as these we are brought to comprehend how the Platonic doctrine of *homoiôsis*, being interpreted through the words of Christ, "he that hath seen me hath seen the Father," acquired a precision and a power which rendered it capable of converting the world.

III. Imitation is the effort of the human will, stirred from its lethargy by the spectacle of our celestial exemplar, to shake itself free of the idolatrous desires of the flesh and to recover its pristine, or native, energy. But the will of man, whatever the cause, is desperately enfeebled, and the heart of man deceitful above all things, and there is no health in us. How shall we, unaided and of our own volition, regain what we have deliberately cast away? It is from thoughts such as these, confirmed seemingly by direct experience, that the Christian has developed the doctrine of grace. The Logos, he believes, did not simply in the Incarnation reveal itself to the logos of man as an inert object to be imitated, but came with power and purpose, with that effluence of the spoken word which passes from person to person and draws them together as it were by invisible bands. We touch here a mystery of psychology as well as of religion which our fumbling science has not yet sounded. We feel the mystic force upon us in our intercourse with men, when familiarity ripens into friendship or beyond friendship into love; we know it as something that goes out of the beloved or admired person, and gradually subdues our spirit to his. And this was what drew the disciples to Jesus when they lived with him in Palestine, drew them with a compulsion of love and homage which seemed to surpass the measure of human influence, and which came to a climax in the ejaculation wrung from the doubting Thomas: "My Lord and my God!"

Nor is this attraction limited to the means of sight and hearing. In the last discourse, recorded by the author of the fourth Gospel, Jesus, wishing to console his disciples, assured them that his going away was even expedient for them, since only so, in the severance of physical ties, should they enjoy fully the purer communion of the spirit:

"And I will pray the Father, and he shall give you another Comforter, that he may abide with you for ever,

"Even the Spirit of truth, whom the world cannot receive, because it seeth him not, neither knoweth him: but ye know him, for he dwelleth with you, and shall be in you."

Jesus was not thinking of a third person in an imaginary Trinity, as his words might at first seem to imply and as they came later to be interpreted (or recast) under the mythopoeic influence of the age. Certainly he was but expressing in vivid metaphorical language the fact that, though he was departing in the body, his spirit should still be with them and in them, as indeed he says explicitly in the very next verse: "I will not leave you comfortless, *I will come to you.*" The thought is exactly the same as that with which the first Gospel concludes: "Lo, I am with you alway, even unto the end of the world." The Holy Ghost, then, is just another name for the Grace of God, whether it be said to proceed from the Father or from the Father and the Son; it is the inner compulsion of spirit upon spirit, of deep calling to deep, by a law of personality of which the outer manifestation is seen in the working of revela-

tion and imitation. And prayer, defined by
Plato and the Fathers as the soul's discourse
with God, would be the voluntary disposition
of the human logos to receive the gracious influence of the divine Logos.

> Sure they do meet, enjoy each other there,
>   And mix, I know not How nor Where.
>   Their friendly Lights together twine,
>   Though we perceive 't not to be so,
>   Like loving Stars which oft combine,
> Yet not themselves their own Conjunctions know.[11]

IV. So far we have considered the economy
as a revelation of the living Logos, with its extension in imitation and grace, but our definition of this last term as the meeting and merging together of twin activities, divine and
human, points to a deeper thought drawn
rather from the death and resurrection than
from the life of Christ,—the thought of redemption as a vicarious atonement. Here confessedly the light is dim, and the Catholic

11 Cowley, *Friendship in Absence*. It should be noted that by
virtue of a certain ambiguity inherent in the Greek mode of
speech the doctrine of grace in the eastern Church never raised
the problem which so much troubled the West. *Charis* means
both a benefit conferred and the gratitude for such a benefit. It
is both active and passive, or, more precisely, like so many similar words in Greek signifies a certain relation or kind of activity between two agents without defining the direction of that
activity; as Sophocles says (*Ajax, 522*), χάρις χάριν γάρ ἐστιν ἡ
τίκτουσ' ἀεί. *Charis* thus implies a mutual activity between God
and man, and there is no place for an antinomy between grace
and faith.

Church has wisely left the matter in the region of pious conjecture without formulating its theories into a creed or fixed dogma. In the West these theories, following the rabbinical temper of St. Paul, have tended to assume the colour of a legalistic or forensic procedure. Sin, from this point of view, is defined as a transgression of the law of God or as an offence against His divine majesty, in either case as a crime punishable by death. And since, for one reason or another, man is incapable of satisfying the requirements of infinite justice, God Himself pays to Himself the penalty by the surrender of His only begotten Son to the ignominy of the Cross, and so redeems the culprit by an act of vicarious atonement. In the East also the view of Christ's death as the purchase price for sin comes up here and there, but commonly with this curious difference. To the Oriental mind it was the devil who must be placated; man by his disobedience has sold himself to the adversary, and Calvary is regarded rather as a ransom paid by God to man's now rightful lord than as a satisfaction to Himself as judge. Occasionally this transaction takes an odd and really immoral slant from what must be deplored as an almost instinctive

admiration among the Greeks for successful
trickery, even swindling. The Son of God by
appearing on earth masked in human form de-
ceives the devil into supposing, and acknow-
ledging, that in the death of this perfect and
representative man he shall have received full
value for his claims, only to find that he has
brought into hell one who is able not merely to
release himself but by his resurrection to de-
liver the world. Satan, as we should say, has
played his trump card, and lost the game,
though, in view of his further machinations, it
cannot be said that he takes his defeat like a
gentleman.

But these were aberrations of fancy that
filtered into the faith from the surrounding
mass of superstition. Behind them lies the feeling that in the Incarnation we see the middle
act of a long drama in which divinity and humanity are enacting their appropriate parts. In
this view the human nature of Christ would be
not *a* man (as indeed it was never so considered
in the orthodox belief), but mankind; and thus,
as symbol or representative or epitome of the
race, or as all three at once (since to the mystical intelligence these three things have a way
of losing their distinction), would be paying the

penalty for the sins of all men once for all. The
beginning of our evil was a turning away from
the light to that darkness wherein were en-
gendered the manifold brood of ruinous illusions. And for us this course, if followed without
check, leads on and on to the extinction of the
logos within us, has in fact already brought us
to the verge thereof. The voluntary death of the
divine Logos in its assumed humanity would
then be a kind of anticipation and prophetic
fulfilment of man's destiny, while the resurrection of humanity by the power of the Logos
would be a guarantee of the victory of man's
spiritual nature over the grave.

Thus, though from one point of view, the
crucifixion may be regarded as only a vivid
consummation of the life of our great exemplar
("And I, if I be lifted up from the earth, will
draw all men unto me"), to the more mystical
eye, and contemplated under the law of sympathy or solidarity which governs the universe
we know not how or why, it would be an act of
vicarious atonement, whereby the incarnate
Logos, taking upon himself the sins of the
world, opens to all fallen souls a door of escape
from the hell of idolatry. To the mind of theologians trained in the subtle ambiguity of

Greek thought, these two views, imitation and redemption, the reaching of the logos from below upwards and its reaching from above downwards, merge together almost indistinguishably in the drama of the divine economy; they are both, in fact, embraced in the Irenaean theory of recapitulation.

So far the records are plain reading. But here and there we come upon suggestions of a play within the play, which the Christians borrowed unwittingly from their gnostic rivals, and never quite forgot, nor yet ever fully admitted. It will be remembered that in the Valentinian mythology the fall and restoration of man had been anticipated by a similar drama among the Aeons of the Pleroma, or, otherwise expressed, were a continuation of the agony of the celestial Sophia. And some relic of that belief, simplified and purified, I seem to detect in such a saying as that of Valentine's critic, Irenaeus: *unum genus humanum, in quo perficiuntur mysteria Dei.*[12] What are these mysteries which can only be carried out in the human

---

[12] *Contra Haer.,* V, xxxvi: *Etenim unus Filius, qui voluntatem Patris perfecit; et unum genus humanum, in quo perficiuntur mysteria Dei, quem concupiscunt angeli videre, et non praevalent investigare sapientiam Dei, per quam plasma ejus conformatum et concorporatum Filio perficitur.*

race, which the angels desire to behold and cannot, to which the doubting frightened eyes of the early believers were directed by the spectacle of a suffering God?

Some notion of what this portent might mean is given by the age-long dispute of theology over the question whether the Incarnation was, as it might be called, an afterthought for the sake of repairing a miscarriage in the original plan of creation, or was purposed from the beginning and so was only incidentally related to the fall of man. This difference of interpretation, discoverable in the writers of the New Testament and carried on through generations of scholars, came to a head among the schoolmen in the contention between the Thomists who supported the former view by such texts as I John iii, 5 and II Peter i, 4, and the Scotists who derived the latter view from the more imaginative language of St. Paul in Ephesians i, 9-12 and Colossians i, 19. In the Occident, so far as I know, the echoes of this ancient battle have long since died away;[13] but in the eastern Church they may still be heard in the debate between such doughty champions of orthodoxy

---

[13] It was, however, still active in the seventeenth century. See Brémond, *Le Sentiment religieux*, IV, 398 ff.

as Androutsos and Rhôssês. "The perfection of
man," says Rhôssês, who holds the more mystical view, "is bound up with the perfecting of
religion, and the necessity of perfecting religion involves necessarily the Incarnation of
the Word of God in that Person in which there
would be not only a perfect imparting of divine
truth, power, and life, but also a perfect human
vehicle to receive this imparted (divine truth,
power, and life). . . . Hence the Incarnation
of the Word would have been necessary for the
perfection of man even without (man's) sin.
Still more did it become necessary because of
the fact of sin, since man did slip into sin by
the wrong use of his reason and free will."[14]
It might be well to stop at this point, nor
search with profane and futile curiosity into
things beyond our utmost comprehension; and
here, in any manner of explicit theorizing, the
orthodox theologians did draw the line. Yet
there is a bare hint now and then, a mere flut-
tering of the veil of silence, indicative of strange
and unacknowledged guesses at the meaning of
the *mysteria Dei*. Such, for instance, are the
halting speculations of Gregory Nyssen and

[14] Rhôssês, Σύστημα Δογματικῆς, 465, quoted by Frank Gavin, *Some
Aspects of Contemporary Greek Orthodox Thought*, 173. For the
contrary view of Androutsos, see his Δογματική, 168.

others, even Athanasius, about the inevitability
of imperfection in the world, owing to the fact
that the very process of creation, as a passage
from what was not to what is, involves change,
and so introduces an element of mutability and
fallibility into the sum of existence. Is this a
cautious way of admitting Plato's *Anankê,*
Necessity, into the universe as a second cause
conditioning the efficiency of the divine cause?
And if the result of creation is from the beginning faulty, what then of the Creator? Is He
without fault? And if the Incarnation with its
tragic climax is no adventitious event imposed
on the creative benevolence by the arbitrary
sinfulness of man, but an integral part of the
.eternal plan, how then? What becomes of the
notion of omnipotence when the will of the omnipotent can be executed only through such
a concession to the need of adversity, and victory is only possible through defeat? *Pathei
mathos,* "by suffering comes wisdom," was said
by Aeschylus, having in mind the fatality that
besets all mortal schemes; must that principle
be extended upward to the deity? We shudder,
perhaps, at such a thought; yet, after all, how
can we think of purpose save in connexion with
obstacles and limitations to the will of him who

purposes? And then, if the dogma of vicarious
atonement leads us to find in the Incarnation
an act of gracious pardon for man's miserable
failure to stand beside his Master as a servant
who has been called to help in the slow and toil-
some task of shaping a cosmos out of chaos,
who perhaps was created to that end, is it also
an appeal to man's pardon—I will not say for
sin, God forbid, but yet for some limitation
there where we should look for perfect strength?
Can there be the least shadow of truth in the
audacious words of the poet,

> For all the Sin wherewith the Face of Man
> Is blacken'd—Man's Forgiveness give—and take?

Long before such an inference the Fathers
of the Church would have drawn back in pious
alarm, and properly, since it springs from a
presumption of knowledge where we are pro-
fessedly ignorant. Yet, on the other hand, the
doctrine of the Logos as the divine purpose fulfilling itself only through sacrifice and suffering must shake our confidence in the smug
commonplaces of theology; the *mysteria Dei*
are not to be clarified by the enumeration of
empty absolutes. We shall believe that in some
way the brief enactment in Palestine, with its
tragic climax on Calvary, is an epitome or sym-

bolic rehearsal of a secular drama at once of creation and redemption wherein the protagonist is God Himself. By the dogma of vicarious atonement the pains and losses and failures of our mortal state become part of a cosmic agony, and any feeling of resentment at the real or seeming injustices of life fades away into awe before the spectacle of the Cross.

In the end we come back to the word "purpose" as decisive of our philosophy and our religion.

Now there are those, and always have been, who fail to perceive in their own consciousness anything more than a vortex of sensations cohering together for a few years about some shadowy centre of gravitation, why no one can guess, and then losing themselves forever in the stream of phenomena that flows on and on to no conceivable goal. To talk of purpose in a world so constituted is mockery. For such men, if they have the courage of their conviction, I do not see what reasonable creed is left but that of the Epicurean: "Let us eat and drink, for tomorrow we die."

Again there are those for whom this visible

universe is no more than an ocean of ephemeral illusions, but who nevertheless have no doubt of a spiritual law holding irresistible and relentless sway in its own separate sphere. The call within to exercise the ethical will is clear and peremptory, yet all the desires and activities connected with this transitory life are frustrate from their inception and end at last in nothing, meaningless all as is the very principle of individual consciousness. For these men I do not see what resting place remains short of the absolute mysticism of India. Purpose, if they are consistent, must be identified by them with a determination to escape utterly from a purposeless existence into some Nirvâna of impersonal timeless bliss, to the nature of which no clue is given by the hopes and fears of the conscious soul in its earthly pilgrimage. Such was the creed put into the mouth of Buddha when he attained to supreme enlightenment under the Bô tree:

> Through many births, a ceaseless round,
> I ran in vain, nor ever found
> The Builder, though the house I saw,—
> For death is born again, and hard the law.
>
> O Builder, thou art seen! not so
> Again thy building shall arise;
> Broken are all its rafters, low

The turret of the mansion lies:
The mind in all-dissolving peace
Hath sunk, and out of craving found release.

And, lastly, there are those who admit no such limitation to the law of purpose, but from all they learn, within and without, infer the being of a divine Builder, whose voice they think they hear calling them to labour with Him in the execution of a great and difficult design. For them this transient life is replete with lessons of infinite purport, and the out-spread glories of this world, through the impediments of imperfection, bear to the discerning eye "authentic tidings of invisible things." These men, whatever their professed creed, belong to the Greek tradition, as followers of Plato and as believers in the incarnate logos; and if they hesitate to associate that belief with the ecclesiastical dogma of Christ the Word, they have at least the *anima naturaliter christiana*.

Certainly Jesus himself taught the doctrine of purpose conceived in the heart of a heavenly Father. The indications of purpose he beheld everywhere, in the beauty of the lily, in the fall of a sparrow, in the destiny of populous cities; and his summoning of men to repentance was to the end that, through a life of purity and humility and love, they might bring their wills into harmony with the will of God, and so be prepared for participation in that kingdom on earth and in heaven of which he, Jesus, presumed to call himself the Lord.

THE END

APPENDIX A

It will be convenient for the lay reader to have before his eye a summary chronology of the principal Greek authors who are drawn upon in the course of this work.

The patristic literature, following the canon of the New Testament, beginning indeed before a few of the later canonical books were written, falls into four quite distinct periods. First come the group of writers commonly designated as Apostolic, or Subapostolic. The chief works of this division are the two *Epistles to the Corinthians* attributed to Clement, third Bishop of Rome (though the second of these Epistles is almost certainly spurious and of a somewhat later date); the Letters of Ignatius, third Bishop of Antioch, written to various churches during his journey to Rome, where he was to suffer martyrdom under Trajan; a Letter of Polycarp, Bishop of Smyrna; an account of the martyrdom of Polycarp in the year 155; the so-called *Didachê*, or manual of church instruction, of doubtful date and origin; the Epistle attributed to Barnabas; a later *Epistle to Diognetus,* and *The Shepherd of Hermas.*

Beginning at a later date but partly contemporary with the Apostolic Fathers is the second group, classed together as the Apologists, who, roughly speaking, wrote within the second and third quarters of the second century. Their task was to defend ("apologize for," in the classical use of the word) the Christian faith and life against the defamations of pagan enemies. The outstanding names are Athanagoras, Theophilus, Tatian, and Justin Martyr.

The third period may be distinguished as that of the Christian Gnostics. It begins with Irenaeus, the Greek Bishop of Lyons, who wrote late in the second century, and includes Clement of Alexandria († after 213) and Origen († 254). Their object, consciously so with Clement and Origen, was to bend Greek philosophy, particularly Platonism, to the service of the new religion in such a manner as to create a Christian *gnôsis* in place of that of the self-styled Gnostics. The movement against which they contended, though it embraced elements of Christianity, should be regarded rather as a rival religion, and a dangerous rival, than a heresy within the Church. Origen also, in his *Contra Celsum,* composed the greatest of the Apologies.

For half a century or more after Origen there is comparative silence, until the opening of the fourth and, as it might be called, classic period, made famous by the great Theologians, or Defenders of Orthodoxy. The notable names here are Athanasius († 373), the three Cappadocians (Basil of Caesarea, his brother Gregory of Nyssa, and their friend Gregory of Nazianzus), and Cyril of Alexandria (though the reputation of the last is not without blemish). Their activity begins with the first General Council held at Nicea in 325 and is consummated, after their death, by the fourth General Council at Chalcedon in 451. Contemporary with them, and preceding them, are a host of writers of varying degrees of orthodoxy and heresy. Their antagonists were within the Church (until excommunicated), and their work was to establish the principles of Christian theology once for all.

The philosophy of Christianity, in the narrower and metaphysical sense of the word, was a production of the following ages, and, unfortunately, took a turn not entirely in harmony with the theological foundation of the Greek Fathers.

APPENDIX B

THE shortest and easiest way to reach a conclusion in regard to the question of the Holy Ghost and the Trinity in the New Testament is to examine the argument of such a treatise as Lebreton's *Dogme de la Trinité,* which is at once thoroughly learned and honest and orthodox, bearing the *imprimatur* of the Roman Church. Now, apart from the trinitarian formula of II Cor. xiii, 13 and Mat. xxviii, 19, which I have discussed in chapter v, the only texts which Lebreton can bring forward from the Bible in support of a *personified* Holy Ghost are the four in the long discourse of Jesus in the fourth Gospel, which in effect have the force of a single passage, as follows:

(a) John xiv, 15-19: "If ye love me, keep my commandments.

"And I will pray the Father, and he shall give you another Comforter, that he may abide with you for ever;

"Even the Spirit of truth; whom the world cannot receive, because it seeth him not, neither knoweth him: but ye know him; for he dwelleth with you, and shall be in you.

"I will not leave you comfortless: I will come to you.

"Yet a little while, and the world seeth me no more; but ye see me: because I live, ye shall live also."

(b) John xiv, 25, 26: "These things have I spoken unto you, being yet present with you.

"But the Comforter, which is the Holy Ghost, whom the Father will send in my name, he shall teach you all things, and bring all things to your remembrance, whatsoever I have said unto you."

(c) John xv, 26: "But when the Comforter is come, whom I will send unto you from the Father, even the Spirit of truth, which proceedeth from the Father, he shall testify of me:"

(d) John xvi, 7-15: "Nevertheless I tell you the truth; It is expedient for you that I go away: for if I go not away, the Comforter will not come unto you; but if I depart, I will send him unto you.

"And when he is come, he will reprove the world of sin, and of righteousness, and of judgement:

"Of sin, because they believe not on me;

"Of righteousness, because I go to my Father, and ye see me no more;

"Of judgement, because the prince of this world is judged.

"I have yet many things to say unto you, but ye cannot bear them now.

"Howbeit when he, the Spirit of truth, is come, he will guide you into all truth: for he shall not speak of himself; but whatsoever he shall hear, that shall he speak: and he will shew you things to come.

"He shall glorify me: for he shall receive of mine, and shall shew it unto you.

"All things that the Father hath are mine: therefore said I, that he shall take of mine, and shall shew it unto you."

Now, in the first place, there is really little or no

strength in the argument commonly put forth that the Spirit is personified because, though the word itself (*pneuma*) is neuter in Greek, the pronouns used of it are masculine. In *a* the relative "whom" and the demonstrative "him" (vs. 17) should properly be "which" and "it"; the neuter form being employed in the Greek because the reference here is closely to *pneuma*, whereas the "Comforter" (*Paraklêtos*, masculine) is thrown in parenthetically. In *b* "whom" (vs. 26) should be "which" (neuter as in the Greek); "he," masculine, is used, since the reference is grammatically to *Paraklêtos*, whereas *Pneuma* is parenthetical. In *c* the English represents the Greek correctly with "whom" and "which" and "he." The point in all three of these passages is that the gender of the pronouns is merely a matter of grammatical agreement, and has no bearing on the question of personification or non-personification.

In *a, b,* and *c* there is no necessary personification. The term Paraklêtos is, I think, properly translated "Comforter." In I John ii, 1 (the only other passage of the New Testament where the word occurs), to be sure, it evidently means "advocate," but such an ambiguous use of a word is more than common in Greek. The verb *parakaleô*, quite idiomatically, has the double sense "to call to another by way of giving aid"; hence *paraklêtos* is one who is called into court to give aid, an *advocatus*, or one who voluntarily gives aid, a comforter. In all three passages (*a, b, c*) the emphasis is on the phrase "the spirit of truth," the inspiration, which, whether from the Father or the Son, will come upon the disciples as the indwelling, invisible memory and presence after the departure of their Master. There is in this no more than the figurative personification common to all poetical language.

The passage *d* does give some warrant for a trinitarian dogma. Particularly the words of vs. 13 ("For he shall not speak of himself; but whatsoever he shall hear, that shall he speak") have the clear ring of personification. But we have no right to take these words alone. We must not dissever them from such a sentence, in the same passage, as this: "A little while, and ye shall not see me," where the coming of the Spirit is manifestly interpreted as the spiritual presence of Christ in the heart. Nor should we forget that in the first epistle of John (admittedly by the same author as the Gospel) the evidence is directly and strongly against any true personification. Consider, for instance, the passage v, 5-8. In our Authorized Version it stands as follows:

"Who is he that overcometh the world, but he that believeth that Jesus is the Son of God?

"This is he that came by water and blood, even Jesus Christ; not by water only, but by water and blood. And it is the Spirit that beareth witness, because the Spirit is truth.

"For *there are three that bear record in heaven, the Father, the Word, and the Holy Ghost: and these three are one.*

"*And* there are three that bear witness *in earth,* the spirit, and the water, and the blood: and these three agree in one."

Now observe that the words here underscored are unquestionably an interpolation made to foist the trinitarian dogma into a passage which originally was too plainly contrary to such a dogma. The interpolated words are found in no Greek manuscript earlier than the fifteenth century; they were unknown to all the Greek Fathers and to the Oriental translators. They are first found in Priscillian, who got them no one knows whence, and in the course of the Middle Ages they gradually worked their way into the Latin text of the Bible. Even Lebreton does not claim that they are authentic. Without this interpolation the spirit is put on precisely the same level as the water and the blood; if one is personified, the other two must be personified. And it is significant of the use of "he" for the Comforter that in this passage "three that bear witness" are masculine in the Greek, though the natural regimen would require the neuter. The Holy Ghost is plainly put on a level with baptism and the eucharist, as the instruments by which we are brought into communion with God.

As for the personal "speak" used of the Spirit in passage *d*, this must be interpreted by such a passage as I Cor. ii, 10-16, where also the Holy Ghost is represented as speaking and teaching, but where, if the Spirit of God is taken to be a person apart from God, by the same reasoning the spirit of man must be held a person apart from the man.

But in the end the personification of the Holy Ghost in the Bible must be rejected not so much because there are no valid arguments for it, as because it deprives the New Testament of its most exquisite and beautiful symbol of the intercommunion of the spirit of God and the spirit of man, for "know ye not that ye are the temple of God, and that the Spirit of God dwelleth in you?"

APPENDIX C

THE question whether Apollinarius really taught the descent of the flesh from heaven is involved in many difficulties, and can only be answered by a careful examination of the texts. To begin with, consider such words as these from his own pen:

"It is rightly confessed that the Lord was a holy birth from the beginning even in the body, and in this is distinguished from every [other] body; for he was not in any way conceived in the womb without divinity, but in union with this. As the angel says, 'The Holy Ghost shall come upon thee and the power of the Highest shall overshadow thee; therefore also that holy thing which shall be born [of thee] shall be called the Son of God'; and it was a celestial descent, not a birth only, this birth from a woman. For not only is it said, 'made (born) of a woman, made (born) under the law,' but also, 'no man hath ascended up to heaven, but he that came down from heaven, even the Son of Man'."[1]

Possibly Apollinarius in these striking words meant to say no more than that by the perfect operation of the *communicatio idiomatum*[2] the body of Christ was so

[1] Lietzmann, *Apollinaris von Laodicea*, 185.
[2] The doctrine of the *communicatio idiomatum*, ἀντίδοσις ἰδιωμάτων, first appears in Tertullian, though it is probably of Greek origin. It became standardized as orthodox, and may be so taken, I suppose, if by the interchange of characteristic traits

assimilated to the Logos at the moment of conception that it might be regarded figuratively, or symbolically, as itself eternal and of heavenly descent. Possibly so; though certainly, taken alone, the phraseology warrants almost demands, a more literal interpretation. The real difficulty arises when we compare such a passage with his repeated denial of its apparent meaning, for instance with his protestation: "It is manifest from what we have always written that no one can bring against us the charges made against some; for we do not say that the flesh of the Saviour was from heaven, nor that the flesh is consubstantial (*homoousios*) with God, according as it is flesh and not God, but only God in so far as it has been united with God into one person."[3] How shall we explain this inconsistency? It may be that the first passage quoted above belonged to an early period before Apollinarius had developed his tripartite psychology and was not acknowledged by him later as representing his true doctrine. It may be that some of his disciples, as commonly happens, went beyond him in the logical development of his theory, or clung to his earlier views after he had changed. In which case it must be remembered that the orthodox theologians were contending not with the man Apollinarius alone (who in fact was generally respected), but with the heresy of which he was the responsible parent. They may have

each party in the transaction (here the divine and human natures of Christ) gains from the other without ceasing to be itself. But at bottom it is a useless excrescence of metaphysics, and I can think of it only in the language applied by Gibbon to the similar doctrine of the περιχώρησις, as "the deepest and darkest corner of the whole theological abyss."

[3] Lietzmann, *op. cit.,* 164.

been careless in distinguishing always between the exact words of the master and the more extravagant inferences drawn by his disciples. But in the main the difficulty arose from the utter confusion in the mind of Apollinarius himself.

A careful study of certain passages from Gregory of Nyssa[4] will show that this confusion was partly linguistic. Apollinarius, as we have seen, divided human nature into three elements: body, soul, and reason (*nous*). Then, having made this trichotomy, he applied the same term "man" at one time to the two elements together of body and soul, at another time to the *nous* alone as the characteristic element, and still again to the three elements combined. If then he said that "the man," as soul and body, was born of Mary and from the earth, that was well so far as the statement went. But if again he spoke of "the man from heaven," meaning thereby the *nous* alone, one can see how the celestial descent of "man" in the latter sense might be transferred to "man" in the former sense, with the result that now the soul and body would be regarded as coming from heaven. The orthodox critics may be censured for overlooking distinctions which Apollinarius desired to maintain; they could retort that he himself was to blame, since he often used language which made the retention of such distinctions impossible. It is not surprising that lovers of plain-speaking should have disregarded his protests and accused him of teaching the descent of the flesh from heaven. If he did not mean this, what did he mean?[5]

4 Lietzmann, *ibid.*, 210 ff.
5 Perhaps the trouble lies in the difficulty of determining

In fact the ambiguity of Apollinarius was not merely verbal. At the back of all this confusion lay the initial fault of attempting to subject the paradox of faith to the canon of Aristotelian logic based on the principle of contradiction, viz. that "the same attribute cannot belong and not belong to the same thing at the same time and in the same respect." But the Incarnation, candidly understood, comes to precisely this contradiction, that the attribute of divinity and the attribute of humanity belong to the same subject, without losing their identity or merging into each other. It may be possible to reconcile this contradiction with the Aristotelian canon, but I suspect that it points rather to an irreconcilable paradox lying as a substratum beneath all the logical superstructure we build about our life. At any rate it was to escape this dilemma that Apollinarius pushed the union of the two natures to their logical extremes, so that in reality they become one nature, neither God nor man, nor yet both together, but a new creature sprung from the mixture of the two. Such at least would be the most straightforward interpretation of what is perhaps the most characteristic passage preserved from his works:

"They abuse us as if we said the flesh was from heaven, when we read the Scriptures which speak of the Son of man from heaven. For when we speak of the Son

whether Apollinarius takes literally or symbolically such texts as John vi, 50, 58, or, if he takes them symbolically, just how he does so. There are not many references in the extant fragments to these verses, but one passage in the *Anakephalaiôsis* (Lietzmann, p. 243) is significant: Οὐδενὸς ἀνθρώπου ἡ σὰρξ ἐξ οὐρανοῦ λέλεκται. Χριστοῦ δὲ ἡ σὰρξ ἐξ οὐρανοῦ εἴρηται· οὐκ ἄρα ἄνθρωπος ὁ Χριστὸς κατὰ τὴν θεότητα τὴν προσλαβοῦσαν τὴν σάρκα. οὕτως οὖν καὶ ἐξ οὐρανοῦ λέγεται διὰ τὸ ἡνῶσθαι τῷ ἐξ οὐρανοῦ.

of God born of a woman, there is no ground for abusing us as if we said the Word was from earth and not from heaven. We say both, viz. that the whole was from heaven because of the Godhead, and that the whole was from a woman because of the flesh, since we know no division of the one person, and neither divide the earthly from the heavenly nor the heavenly from the earthly."[6]

In the end the logic of Apollinarius brings us back to the old metaphysical fallacy of the absolute infinite and the absolute finite. God the Father is lifted into perfect isolation from the world; the Son ceases to be a mediator embracing both divinity and humanity in harmonious conjunction, and becomes a kind of nondescript intermediary between the two.[7] And again we have the curious fact that heresies springing from different, even contrary, sources run together at the last; for this intermediary of Apollinarius is practically the same as the secondary God of the Arians whom he had set out to confute.

It may or may not be precise to say that Apollinarius taught the descent of Christ's body from heaven—virtually, or inferentially, if you will, he certainly did so teach—but to accuse the Cappadocians of setting up a man of straw and attacking it slanderously in the name of Apollinarius is, I am bound to think, to show a deficient sense of historical conditions.

6 Lietzmann, *op. cit.*, 259.
7 Cf. Lietzmann, frags. 107, 113; and see Athanasius, *Contra Ar.*, ii, 26 on the nature of the μεσίτης.